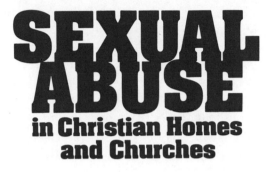

# SEXUAL ABUSE

## in Christian Homes and Churches

# Video Resource Available

Author Carolyn Holderread Heggen is featured in an interview on a video, **Beyond the News . . . Sexual Abuse.** She talks frankly about her counseling experiences with survivors of sexual abuse, many of whom came from "very religious" homes.

If you are considering a group study of *Sexual Abuse in Christian Homes and Churches* or want to know more about the issue, you may want to obtain this video. You will hear true stories told by survivors of sexual abuse—date rape, child abuse, abuse by leaders in the church, and from a perpetrator of date rape.

**Beyond the News . . . Sexual Abuse** is produced by Mennonite Media Ministries, 1251 Virginia Avenue, Harrisonburg, VA 22801. You may contact them for more information or to purchase this and other videos at 1 800 999-3534. You may also order **Beyond the News . . . Sexual Abuse** from Provident Bookstore by calling 1 800 759-4447.

# SEXUAL ABUSE
## in Christian Homes and Churches

### CAROLYN
### HOLDERREAD
### HEGGEN

Foreword by
Marie M. Fortune

HERALD PRESS
Scottdale, Pennsylvania
Waterloo, Ontario

**Library of Congress Cataloging-in-Publication Data**
Heggen, Carolyn Holderread, 1946-
    Sexual abuse in Christian homes and churches / Carolyn Holderread
Heggen.
        p.   cm.
    Includes bibliographical references.
    ISBN 0-8361-3624-1 (alk. paper)
    1. Adult child sexual abuse victims—Pastoral counseling of.
2. Sexually abused children—Pastoral counseling of. 3. Child
molesting—Religious aspects—Christianity. 4. Child molesting—
Prevention. 5. Sex—Religious aspects—Christianity. I. Title.
BV4464.3.H43  1993
261.8'32—dc20                                                92-32143
                                                                   CIP

The Bible text is from the *New Revised Standard Version Bible,* copyright ©
1989, by the Division of Christian Education of the National Council of
the Churches of Christ in the USA, and is used by permission.

Scripture quotation marked NASB is from the New American Standard
Bible, © The Lockman Foundation 1960, 1962, 1963, 1968, 1971, 1972,
1973, 1975, and is used by permission.

SEXUAL ABUSE IN CHRISTIAN HOMES AND CHURCHES
Copyright © 1993 by Herald Press, Scottdale, Pa. 15683
    Published simultaneously in Canada by Herald Press,
    Waterloo, Ont. N2L 6H7. All rights reserved
Library of Congress Catalog Number: 92-32143
International Standard Book Number: 0-8361-3624-1
Printed in the United States of America
Book design and cover art by Gwen M. Stamm

1 2 3 4 5 6 7 8 9 10 02 01 00 99 98 97 96 95 94 93

*To my courageous friends
in the Network of Adult Survivors of Abuse.*

# Contents

# Foreword

In *Texts of Terror*, Phyllis Trible asks us to recall and reflect on some of the most painful stories in Scripture: accounts of sexual violence and abuse. Trible calls us to remember the victims whose truth these texts tell. She asks us to recall Tamar, the Unnamed Concubine, and others, and to recognize that their stories are ours.

The betrayal of trust, exploitation of vulnerability, and physical and emotional suffering the biblical accounts reveal are not merely ancient metaphors. They are the lived experiences of many people in our families and churches. As Carolyn Holderread Heggen so clearly and movingly documents in *Sexual Abuse in Christian Homes and Churches,* the history of our churches is rife with denial of the common experience of sexual abuse. And when churches have acknowledged abuse at all, they have stigmatized the survivor who dares to disclose the abuse.

A woman discovered her husband sexually abusing their two children. She had him arrested and did her best to protect her children from further harm. Then she turned to her church for help. She could no longer, the church said, teach Sunday school, and her children—the victims—could no longer attend. The church said nothing to the perpetrator husband, also a church member.

This woman's church punished her for trying to be a good parent protecting her children. The church refused to confront and hold the offender accountable. Unfortunately, such incidents are not unusual. Sexual violence and abuse take place in a patriarchal context, in settings in which men dominate and women submit. The most common victims are women as well as children of both genders.

This is no surprise, since patriarchy continues to regard women and children as property of men. Women have less power than men in every measurable social, economic, and political category. We are vulnerable to the power and control of men—and are most vulnerable to the men closest to us.

Sexual abuse is one of the most concrete means of exercising power and control over someone else. In such abuse the misuse of power to control and dominate others is inextricably tied to the reinforcement of erotic stimulation for the offender. This creates a complex web of power and eroticism difficult to untangle. Changing the behavior of sexual abusers is difficult and sometimes impossible.

Sexual violence and abuse in a patriarchal setting are socially accepted, tolerated, and sanctioned. Yes, there are laws against it. But convictions are hard to come by. The voices speaking out against these common atrocities come mostly from the margins, not the center. The norm, despite our best efforts, is the sexual abuse of women and children by men is an extension of male privilege.

In contrast to this tendency for abuse by men to be tolerated, a woman offender is likely to receive severe punishment. Sexual abuse by women, especially of children, is not acceptable. Not only has she abused her child, perhaps more importantly she has exercised a male prerogative. Indeed she must be punished. Because we live in a patriarchy, abuse perpetrated by men is far more common and less likely to be confronted. This has created a vast and tragic social problem.

The church, past and present, has accepted and promoted a patriarchal agenda. In its teaching, practice, exegesis, and preaching, the church has perpetuated an ideology about men, women, and children in general—and about sexuality and abuse in particular—which has sustained the very foundation of the widespread problem of sexual violence.

The church has for a generation invested enormous time, money, and people resources on blanket condemnations of "the sin of homosexuality." If the church had instead identified the sin of sexual abuse and made a commitment to change the social norms which support it, we would be much farther along in efforts to eradicate sexual abuse and violence. But homophobia, combined with a deep and abiding denial of the reality of abuse and unwillingness to challenge this male prerogative, have prevented adequate response.

For every minister who says, "But no one ever comes to me with this problem!" there are dozens of victims, survivors, and perpetrators who desperately need the ministry of the church. Whether through passive denial or active efforts to silence victims and survivors, the church contradicts its own mandate to justice. The response of the church to sexual abuse has been a prime example of *religion in service to patriarchy.*

The church has within it the resources to name and confront sexual abuse. In fact, Scripture mandates the church to stand with those who are objects of harm and exploitation, to protect the little ones, to offer hospitality to the vulnerable, to set free those imprisoned by social convention. Jesus' ministry with women and children provides an unequivocal model of justice-making as the appropriate response to the injustices heaped on the oppressed.

Finally, like a sleeping giant, the church is waking to the problem of sexual abuse. After centuries of denial of incest, rape, and sexual harassment, the church is now responding to the most recent disclosure of abuse—sexual abuse by clergy within their ministrial relationships. Some in institutional church leadership are genuinely concerned to address a problem seriously undermining the credibility of the entire church.

Other leaders are offering a halfhearted response under duress—legal liability and enormous financial costs are forcing recognition of the longstanding problem of abuse by clergy.

However, even institutional self-interest is helping to open a door which may allow voices of all victims and survivors to be heard.

The challenge remains that expressed by Trible in her essay on the Judges 19 story of the Levite and his Unnamed Concubine, who are overnight guests in the home of a villager. When a gang of men threatens to assault the Levite, he fearfully tosses his concubine over the threshold to the gang, then locks the door. The men brutally rape and beat the concubine, leaving her for dead. Next morning the Levite opens the door and finds her there.

On which side of the threshold will the church stand? That is the question both Trible and this searing book by Carolyn Holderread Heggen ask us to ponder. Will we stand safely behind locked doors, with the powerful determined to protect male privilege and sacrifice the marginal persons? Or will we stand with the victims outside the safety of the locked door?

We are the church. The choice is ours.

—Marie M. Fortune, author of
*Sexual Violence: The Unmentionable
Sin* and *Is Nothing Sacred?* and
director of the Center for the
Prevention of Sexual and
Domestic Violence
Seattle, Washington

# Preface

When I became a psychotherapist in the mid-1970s, I did not suspect that my practice would one day consist mostly of adult survivors of sexual abuse. Throughout graduate training I heard not one lecture or discussion on the incidence or resultant issues of childhood sexual abuse. Even in my secular universities, incest seemed too repugnant to discuss.

So it was with great surprise that I found client after client sharing stories of childhood sexual victimization by parents or siblings, grandparents, aunts or uncles, cousins or trusted family friends. Equally disturbing as the frequency with which I heard the accounts was the fact that many survivors described their homes as "very religious" or "Christian." They often termed their abusers "godly," "devout," or "Christian" people.

Victims whose families were involved in church often told of futile childhood attempts to let someone within the congregation know. Trying in adulthood to share their story and pain, victims frequently encountered awkward and alienating responses from church people. Some sympathetic church members were sincere but ineffectual in their efforts to walk with survivors working at adult recovery.

Many Christians now know that sexual abuse among church families is indeed a problem. But few church members or leaders understand the dynamics of abuse or know how to minister effectively to victims. Few know how to intervene redemptively in currently abusing families. Few know how to work toward the prevention of sexual abuse or how to help congregational members develop healthy sexual attitudes and behaviors.

This book grows out of my own journey of healing. Its purpose is to give congregations, clergy, and lay people the knowledge and tools to become effective channels of healing and grace for victims, perpetrators, families, and congregations wounded by sexual abuse. I hope this book will help equip the church to work for the prevention of further abuse and the development of healthy sexuality.

There are both female and male victims and perpetrators of abuse. However, there is general agreement among researchers and mental health professionals that the offender is predominantly male and the victim predominantly female. As a reflection of this gender distribution and not because of linguistic sexism, offenders will be referred to with masculine pronouns and abuse survivors with feminine pronouns.

While this book focuses primarily on male offenders and female victims, I acknowledge that many males also have been victimized, and they likewise face severe and destructive consequences. But as a woman whose primary clinical and research work has been with other female victims, I will not attempt to explain the experience of male victimization. It is a story which needs to be told—but by a man.

You needn't start at the beginning of this book and proceed chronologically to the end. If you come to a chapter which doesn't engage you, skip to a chapter you find more interesting. If you find you have a low tolerance for the topics discussed in this book, I urge you at least to read chapters 7 (Repentance, Restitution, Forgiveness, and Reconciliation), 10 (Preventing Sexual Abuse) and 11 (Congregational Role in Developing Healthy Sexuality) before tossing the book aside.

I owe you, the reader, several warnings before you continue. If you are a perpetrator of abuse and have not confessed your sin and begun to heal, this book may evoke deep emotional anxiety and shame. Find a friend, pastor, or professional with whom you can talk and begin the steps toward repentance and healing.

If you are a victim of sexual abuse, reading this book may stir up frightening memories and feelings. Share these reactions with someone. This is not a self-help book for recovery from abuse. You will need the support and safety which a compassionate friend or trained professional can provide. If you have no one with whom to talk about these feelings, ask your pastor for a suggestion, or call a rape crisis center, local women's bookstore, women's resource center, or women's shelter for the names of available resources.

If books were classified as movies are, this book would need to carry at least an "R" rating. This is not so much because it talks about explicit sexual matters (which it does) but particularly because it deals with profound and explicit violence—violence to the body, the spirit, and the heart of the abused.

I deeply admire all who have survived this abusive assault to both body and soul. A special salute goes to those who not only have survived but are thriving, turning woundedness and pain into beauty and strength. Compassion and understanding extend to those victims who didn't make it—to those for whom the pain and despair and hopelessness were insurmountable and, in some cases, fatal.

While I have been highly committed to this book, the project is not mine. It belongs, rather, to all who have found courage to face the pain of their abusive past. I am deeply grateful to the hundreds of survivors of sexual abuse who have shared their stories with me in clinical settings, in research projects, in hallways after workshops and lectures, and informally over tea. I am particularly grateful to those who gave me permission to use their true stories. Their accounts and quotes enrich this book in ways that theoretical abstractions never could. I am also grateful to those who, writing from their personal journeys, generously shared prayers, litanies, and poems for inclusion.

I salute the courage and commitment to truth telling which Herald Press shows by publishing this book. Michael King has been a sensitive, wise guide, and a friend throughout the writing process; I never dared hope for all this in an editor. Arbutus Sider, Willard Krabill, Joan King, Cathryn Passmore, Scott Walker, and Joyce Munro read the original manuscript. This is a better book because of their insightful suggestions.

I am indebted to Marie Fortune. She not only read, critiqued, and wrote the foreword for this manuscript; she has been a mentor and source of encouragement to many of us working for justice in Christian homes and churches. Kristina Mast Burnett of Mennonite Central Committee's Women's Concerns has been an important resource and advocate for this project as well as survivors' concerns in general. The Schowalter Foundation supported the project with a financial grant.

Thank you to numerous friends who have sustained me in so many ways during this time. You've helped me laugh and hope when I couldn't on my own. My husband, Richard, provided important technical assistance with the intimidating machinery of modern word processing. More importantly, he supported this undertaking each step of the way. I'm grateful to him and my three children for understanding how much this project mattered to me and the church. Good news, kids—I'm ready to start baking cookies and going rollerblading again!

If books have matron saints, Clarice Kratz is indeed the saint behind this project. Sharing in the church her story of abuse and healing, she began to break down my denomination's wall of secrecy and denial and provides a model of healing and grace for other survivors.

—*Carolyn Holderread Heggen*
*Albuquerque, New Mexico*

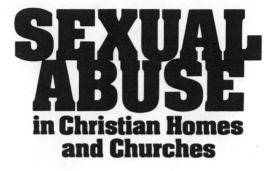

# SEXUAL ABUSE

## in Christian Homes and Churches

# Chapter 1

# Sexual Abuse: What Is It and Why Is It Wrong?

If you are like me, you may have skipped over the preface of this book and jumped right into this first chapter. If so, because of important words of warning in the preface, I urge you to turn back and read the preface.

A three-year-old girl is visiting her grandparents. While Grandma is in town, Grandpa asks the little girl to undress. She is perplexed but complies. He looks at her and masturbates. Is this sexual abuse?

A five-year-old boy is left in the care of his brother, age fifteen. The older brother suggests they take a bath. While they are in the tub together, the older brother fondles his little brother's genitals and asks him to do the same to him. The younger brother is embarrassed and baffled. Has he been sexually abused?

The father of a ten-year-old-girl comes into her bedroom to kiss her good night. He puts his hands on her cheeks, holding her face firmly in place while he kisses her deeply. His thrusting tongue causes her embarrassment and physical discomfort. She tries to avoid his kisses by pretending she is asleep. Is he sexually abusing her?

A fourteen-year-old girl awakens in the middle of the night to find hands fondling her breasts. Opening her eyes, she sees her father bending over her, hands under her nightgown. Has she been sexually abused?

A thirty-five-year-old mentally impaired woman lives in a group home. A young social worker who coordinates heath care for the residents brings her stuffed animals and chocolate candy in exchange for her posing nude for him and her promise that she'll never tell. He photographs her and hangs the photos in his apartment bedroom. Is this sexual abuse?

A middle-aged single woman receives pastoral counseling at her church. The pastor tells her that until she gets over her "hang-ups" about men she'll never have an intimate relationship with God. He includes intimate kisses and embraces as part of her counseling. Is this abusive?

An elderly woman with Alzheimer's disease is bedfast in a church-operated nursing home. The director periodically comes into her room and locks the door. He doesn't remove either her clothing or his but lays on top of her, masturbating to orgasm. She tries to tell the nursing staff he is doing bad things to her but people assume she is confused. Has she been sexually abused?

These vignettes are all true. In each case the perpetrator was a professing Christian. In each case I believe sexual abuse did occur. Why?

Sexual abuse occurs whenever anyone with less maturity or power is tricked, trapped, coerced, or bribed into a sexual experience. It occurs whenever anyone disempowered by handicap, age, or situation is involved in an activity which is sexually stimulating to the perpetrator and which the victim does not fully comprehend or to which she is unable to give informed consent. The imbalance of power between victim and perpetrator is critical in the determination of abuse. The power imbalance may result from the perpetrator's greater age, size, position, experience, or authority.

Most sexual abuse does not involve physical violence. Rather, it usually involves some form of coercion and a misrepresentation of the activity. Coercion is fueled by the perpetrator's desire for secrecy, which is necessary to prevent intervention and to allow him continued access to the victim.

Tragically, sexual abuse victims are both young and old. The therapeutic community has long known the vulnerability of children to abuse. Now we are becoming aware of the frequency with which elderly people are being sexually victimized. Due to physical limitations, some of the elderly cannot protect themselves from unwanted sexual contact. Because of the effects of senility or other mental impairment, some may not be able psychologically to defend themselves. Case studies indicate that when elderly persons accuse a caregiver of abuse, they are rarely believed and are instead frequently discredited as "senile" or "incompetent."

Physically and mentally challenged people of all ages are another population vulnerable to sexual abuse. Limited verbal skills may make it difficult for such persons to describe their mistreatment. Elderly or handicapped persons may be ill, isolated, and fearful that there is no other place for them to go. Often this is indeed true. Abusers often target the elderly and handicapped because they sense their victims' vulnerability.

In sexual abuse, the needs and wishes of the victim are ignored. The victim is instead used for the sexual gratification and stimulation of the abuser. This may involve intercourse, touching of breasts or genitalia, or exposure to sights or sounds sexually stimulating to the perpetrator.

Some people assume that intercourse or some form of genital contact must occur before an activity can be called sexual abuse. Current understandings, however, are that sexual abuse can occur without physical touch. Personal physical and emotional space may be violated through words, sounds, or exposure to sights which are sexual in nature.

Some people assume that sexual abuse which involves intercourse or genital contact is more damaging than other abuse. Research and clinical evidence do not consistently substantiate this. All abusive sexual experiences can cause damage and long-term pain which eventually must be faced and healed lest it cause ongoing emotional trauma.

There are several types of abuse. Sexual abuse may involve *physical contact*. This includes fondling of the victim's breasts or genitals, sexual kissing, forcing the victim to touch the perpetrator's genitals, intercourse, and oral or anal sex. This is the category which usually comes to people's minds when they think of sexual abuse.

But there are other important categories of abusive behavior. Sexual abuse may be *verbal*. One woman in her fifties still remembers the way her father took great interest in her developing breasts. As they changed in size he called them her peanuts, then her walnuts, and finally her coconuts. Jokes were made at the family table about her breasts. Her father would inspect her outfit every morning to see if it was too revealing of her feminine figure. "He acted as though he owned my breasts and as though they were designed for his pleasure. Although he never touched them, his commenting on them made me feel as violated as if he had touched them."

Another woman remembers her grandfather holding her on his lap and whispering in her ear seductive, sexual comments about her "pretty, juicy lips" and "cute little breasts." At the time she didn't understand why this was so terrifying to her, but as an adult she realizes how vulnerable and violated she felt.

Sexual abuse may be *visual*. One woman remembers the dread she felt whenever her family would go to a certain uncle's home. This uncle would pull her into a bedroom and lock the door. Then he would bring out pornographic magazines and force her to look at the photos. Although he never touched her, he would watch her and masturbate as she embarrassedly looked at the photos.

An adult woman recalls the shame she felt as a teenager when her father pulled the bath towel off her body as she walked from the shower to her bedroom. He left her standing naked and humiliated before him.

Another woman recalls the fear and repulsion she felt as an adolescent when her father would expose his nude body to her. This same father also walked into her bedroom or the bathroom without knocking. When he found her undressed on such occasions, she would scream and tell him to get out. He would stare at her private body parts and laugh before leaving. When she finally got the courage to talk to her mother about this, the mother's response was: "Don't be so sensitive; it's only your father, after all."

Exhibitionism, or "indecent exposure," as it is often called, is widely considered a criminal act. It appears that exposure to the nude sexual body parts of a stranger causes less psychological trauma than exposure with sexual intentions by a father, other family member, or trusted friend.

A woman in her 60s, who has been married for almost forty years and has raised three sons, confides that she still cannot see her husband's nude body without fear and revulsion. When she was a young girl, her preacher-father would periodically come into her room, drop his pants, and force her to look at his erect penis. Almost fifty years later, she still vividly recalls feeling terrorized and nauseated when this happened. "The same feelings still wash over me whenever I see my dear, gentle husband's nude body."

Sexual abuse may be *psychological*. This category of abuse occurs when a parent behaves in ways which blur the appropriate emotional boundary between a parent and child. Sometimes a child is set up as a surrogate spouse and confidant. While children may feel flattered to be so special to parents, children become confused when told things they may instinctively know are appropriate only between married people. Frequently a subtle sexual dynamic becomes part of the surrogate spouse-parent relationship. Even though the sexual dynamic may not be overtly acted out, it causes confusion and an inappropriate sexual bonding between child and parent.

One woman tells of the trauma she experienced as a young adolescent when her father would come to her bedroom to talk about "what men like from women in bed." He knew she was sexually inexperienced but said he was doing her future husband a big favor by grooming her to be a good lover. He would use his own sexual relationship with her mother as an example of how frustrating it was for a man to be married to a woman with "sexual hang-ups."

Even though the daughter begged him to stop talking to her

about these things, he persisted over several years. When she threatened to tell her mother, he convinced her that because of "mother's hang-ups about these things" she would divorce him if she knew he was giving the daughter "private lessons." Not wanting to be the cause of divorce, she never told. The adult daughter today understands that "even though he never once touched me inappropriately, I realize I am the victim of psychological incest."

I am frequently asked, usually by frightened parents who have found young children involved in sexual play, to clarify the difference between sexual abuse and normal sexual play among children. It is an important question. It is normal for children to be curious about their own and other children's bodies. It is normal for children to touch their own bodies and other children's bodies in ways that feel pleasurable. In this way children learn about their bodies and what they like and don't like.

If the children are approximately the same age and size and neither coercion, trickery, nor intimidation are involved, this is normal sexual play. But if an older sibling, baby-sitter, or other child with perceived authority engages a less powerful child in sexual behavior which the younger child does not understand and feels unable to decline, this is abusive.

Sometimes children of about the same age have significant differences in ego strength and personality forcefulness. Their are situations in which children of the same age are unequal in their sense of personal strength and authority. In such situations the less forceful child may be coerced into activities accurately considered abusive.

## Why Is Sexual Abuse Wrong?

Unfortunately, one can't find specific biblical references which prohibit sexual abuse of children by fathers. Leviticus passages which speak to sexual prohibitions for the Hebrews refer to sexual contact between a man and a female considered the property of another man. Many relationships are identified as inappropriate for sexual relations—son and mother, nephew and aunt, father and granddaughter, brother and sister, and on and on. Blatantly missing is a prohibition against father and daughter or father and son sexual contact. The Leviticus prohibitions appear to reflect more concern for the property rights of men than concern for the exploitation of vulnerable people.

Marie Fortune, ordained minister and director of the Seattle-based Center for the Prevention of Sexual and Domestic Violence, provides clear Christian comment on abusive behavior. Her insights are particularly helpful as we attempt to understand why sexual abuse is wrong.

Fortune (1983) observes that sexual abuse is a multidimensional sin. It is a *bodily sin* which violates the body integrity of the abused and results in lifelong body-related issues for the victim. It is a *relational sin* which violates trust and destroys the possibility of a healthy relationship between the victim and the abused. It likewise makes it difficult for the victim to trust others and thus impedes all other current and future relationships. It is a *social sin* because it thrives in secretive situations which sustain abusive relationships and create a destructive environment. Even those not directly involved are affected by the abuse of a family, church, or community member.

And abuse is a *sexual sin* because it distorts and misuses sexuality. Abuse damages the victim's feelings about sexuality and leaves her with aftereffects which will change her ability to accept and express her sexuality long after the abuse has ended.

Fortune says that in terms of a theology of creation in which humans are affirmed as creatures made in God's own image, acts of sexual abuse are blasphemous because they deny the sacredness of another human being. In ordinary words, sexual abuse is wrong because it hurts people and causes them lifelong scars! The following chapter examines these scars.

## Chapter 2
# The Victim and Resultant Issues

Some people suspect the problem of sexual abuse has been blown out of proportion. They believe abuse is the media's latest pet sensation or pop psychology's new blame-all. A pastor recently said, "I'm getting sick and tired of therapists trying to dredge up a history of sexual abuse in every woman they see!"

Others express frustration that women who have had unwanted, inappropriate sexual experiences as children "make such a big deal out of it. After all, it was only a small part of her childhood. Why doesn't she concentrate on the good things that happened?" Others may exclaim, "She's just using this as an excuse to feel sorry for herself and get people's pity." Several women report having heard pastors use the biblical story of Lot's wife (who turned into a pillar of salt when she looked backward) as a warning of the inappropriateness of "looking back," of thinking too much about one's past.

The therapeutic community now realizes that surviving sexual abuse is in many ways like surviving war. Survivors on both fronts may suffer from post-traumatic stress disorder (PTSD).

This disorder involves a cluster of characteristic symptoms which develop following a psychologically distressing event that is outside the usual range of human experience.

Symptoms of PTSD may include amnesia, nightmares, and disturbing flashbacks. Memories are selective and muted. But flashbacks are intense bits of memories which bring back all the terror of the original event. Many find that once the flashbacks begin there is no way of stopping them. This poem describes the painful process of remembering long-repressed traumatic childhood events.

### I Remember

*by Ann Campbell*

> I remember things, Lord,
> and I hurt all over again.
> A quivering child,
> monstrous hands
> grasping—groping
> muffled cries pleading with the darkness,
> stab through me
> bringing memories
> like gaping wounds.
> I hurt all over again.
> Heal me, Lord.
> Wash my wounds away
> as rain gently cleanses
> the dust
> from the flower,
> That I might be healed
> and full of your glory.

Many working in the field of mental health believe nothing in childhood can so profoundly hinder emotional and spiritual well-being as having been sexually abused by someone known and trusted. Sexual abuse is a violation of the body, of personal boundaries, and of trust. It destroys a sense of personal, individual value. It objectifies persons—treats them as objects, as things.

No wonder sexual abuse is sometimes called "murder of the soul."

Most adult survivors of abuse have put such emotional energy into mere day-to-day survival that until they begin therapy they are unaware of the ongoing effects of their childhood abuse. Instead, victims may have a sense of vague anxiety, of generalized emotional pain and sadness which permeates everything they do and every relationship in which they become involved.

Why is childhood sexual abuse such a devastating experience for victims? What are the aftereffects and adulthood issues for the abused?

This chapter will explore the world of the survivor. It will look at varied and creative ways victims try to protect themselves from the psychological pain of abuse. It will explore resultant issues related to self-blame and self-esteem, to the body, to relationships, and to faith and spirituality. Because human nature is complex and multifaceted, no two people respond in exactly the same way to life experiences. But there are common themes and challenges that arise in the lives of survivors.

## Self-Protective Defense Mechanisms

Most survivors of childhood sexual abuse who have not undergone their own healing journey are unaware of the profound effect of their victimization. They tend to discredit its significance. "It happened so many years ago." "Worse things have happened to so many others." "My life was never in danger so it couldn't have been such a big deal. I think I've just exaggerated the whole thing in my mind."

If the abused child feels fully the fear and rage associated with her abuse, she will go crazy. She can not survive emotionally as a helpless child in a hostile, dangerous home unless she denies the painful reality of her experience. When intolerable trauma is inflicted on a human being, the person must do something to make it more tolerable, more manageable. Sometimes this leads to a gross distortion of the reality which may be too painful to face.

Defense mechanisms are ways of changing or distorting reality to reduce anxiety, fear, and stress. Freud was the first to observe that people distort reality to protect themselves from emotional pain. Although each defense mechanism operates differently, there are two common characteristics of defenses. First, they are denials or distortions of reality. Second, they usually operate unconsciously.

Because childhood sexual abuse is such a stressful, anxiety-producing experience, survivors generally use several defense mechanisms to help them cope. These defenses keep victims unaware of the true depth of their woundedness.

*Denial* is perhaps the simplest of all defense mechanisms. In denial the victim defends herself against the pain of facing her abuse by "closing her eyes" to indications and memory fragments of victimization. If she recalls Dad coming into her bed at night and fondling her, she restructures the memory and believes she was only dreaming. Denial allows her to rewrite her personal history, to restructure painful events and thus fabricate her own more acceptable reality. As children, denial keeps many victims from telling anyone about their abuse; as adults, denial prevents their facing their victimization and resultant pain.

*Repression* is a defense mechanism which keeps unpleasant feelings and memories from coming into conscious awareness. It is the involuntary removal of something painful from consciousness. Through repression many victims of childhood abuse maintain the fantasy that they came from wonderful homes and had perfect childhoods. When she hears of sexual abuse in others, the victim using repression can say sincerely, although falsely, " Thank God, it never happened to me!"

*Rationalization* involves a reinterpretation of behavior to make it seem more acceptable. Rationalization makes up acceptable excuses for behaviors that cause anxiety. Survivors frequently have convincing explanations for why someone abused them. "He didn't realize it was me he was fondling; he thought I was Mother. You see, he always did have a problem with sleepwalking." Or, as another woman explained to me, "He only abused me when he was drunk or under a lot of stress. He never did those things to me unless there was a good reason."

Healing requires the strength and safety to experience the

feelings which have so long been suppressed. Defenses allowed the child to minimize her perceptions of the pain of abuse. But healing requires that she feel her feelings and reclaim her lost memories.

I am often asked, "Why bring up all those painful memories again? Isn't it better just to let people forget their past if it was so unhappy?" If it were truly possible to forget childhood trauma and to live healthy, happy lives without facing early wounds, I would surely agree. But it takes great energy to keep defenses up and past trauma down. The energy needed to keep emotional pain repressed is not available for other things that we need and want to do to live happy, loving lives.

Even though memories may be hidden away in the unconscious, they have tremendous energy and power. They try in multiple ways to get our attention, to tell us there is emotional work which must be done. Ignoring these memories won't work forever. They may invade our dream life with recurring, sometimes frightening fragments of information about unfinished business which needs attention. Buried anger or pain may leak out at inappropriate times in tears, screams, or tantrum. Repressed rage may spew forth in surprising fits of anger; we may sincerely say, "Now where did that come from?"

In more subtle but equally significant ways, denied pain and buried memories affect our daily lives. Our ability to be in healthy relationships with ourselves, others, and God is inextricably tied to early experiences and childhood relationships with primary caretakers. Childhood sexual abuse demands to be faced and can't be indefinitely ignored without causing severe emotional, relational, and spiritual damage.

## Self-Blame and Resultant Self-Esteem Issues

Victims of sexual abuse who have not begun their healing journeys often fail to see the connection between past abuse and present poor functioning. Many express surprise or disbelief that so many of the problems they face may in fact be related to their abuse. As one survivor says,

I always thought that I was the problem, that I had done something terrible which I couldn't remember but for which I was being punished by having to carry around this terrible pain in my heart. Whatever I had done was surely the reason for my long history of depression, eating disorders, self-abusive behaviors, and broken relationships.

Children's survival depends on the adults in their lives. To acknowledge that the very people responsible for their care and nurture are violent and abusive terrifies children. If they cannot trust family and relatives to have their best interests at heart and to keep them safe, what hope is there for survival in this world?

It is "easier" for a child to assume that parents aren't really cruel and untrustworthy and that the abuse is really her fault. Self-blame decreases her sense of powerlessness and vulnerability. She knows it is impossible to change the world or the adults in it. However, she may find some hope in believing that if she could be different (maybe less attractive, more alert, or purer in heart), she could be spared further abuse. So the child assumes responsibility and takes on the sins of her abuser in an unconscious attempt to feel less vulnerable.

As I work with adult survivors, I am often amazed at the strong inclination many still have to blame themselves for their childhood abuse. Victims feel guilty for somehow having caused the abuse or for not having been able to stop it. "I guess I was too pretty," says one victim. "I probably developed physically too young—before I was mature enough to know how to defend myself," says another. "If I had been more courageous I would have run away, but I've always been spineless." "I was too embarrassed and shy to tell anyone what was happening, so I have no one but myself to blame."

While self-blame is a common defense against feelings of utter powerlessness for child victims, it becomes destructive when carried into adulthood. Many adult survivors still believe that because they feel guilty, they *are* guilty. And because they feel unworthy, they *are* unworthy.

This exaggerated sense of personal responsibility for victimization becomes part of the personality structure of many victims. Throughout life victims may struggle with an unhealthy tendency to accept blame and responsibility not appropriately theirs. Many victims were told by their abusers that the abuse was their fault. "I know you really want me to be doing this to you, so that's why I'm doing it." "If you didn't dress so sexy this would never have happened. What do you expect? I'm only human." "If you didn't upset and depress your mom so much, I could be getting this from her."

Because child victims wrongly assumed they were the only ones to whom sexual abuse was happening, they felt isolated and different. Many tell of feeling as though they had an indelible mark on their forehead which made it easy for everyone to look at them and know what was happening. "Once the abuse started," says one survivor, "I felt too ashamed to look anyone directly in the eye because I was sure they could tell what my father was doing to me. I couldn't even look at my own eyes in the mirror without crying and feeling overcome by shame."

Another survivor believed she had fallen to earth from another planet. "What else could explain the fact that I felt so different and isolated from other girls my age?" The following poem, written just before a suicide attempt, conveys the sense of loneliness and isolation many victims feel.

> Where are you going, little girl?
>     i am alone
> Where are you going, little girl?
>     i am alone
> Why are you crying, little girl?
>         i have no place to go
>         i am alone
> What have you seen, little girl?
>     i am blind
> What do you know, little girl?
>             no one can touch me
>             i am alone
>             no one can see me
>             i am alone
>         there's no one here

Survivors who didn't try to resist the sexual advances of their abusers or who accepted gifts and privileges in exchange for sexual favors may be particularly prone to deep shame as adults. An ongoing and haunting question for them may be, "Why didn't I stop him?" Even comparing the physical size and strength of a 60-pound child with that of a 175-pound man may not convince the survivor that holding off her abuser was unlikely. It is difficult for the victim to believe that whatever the circumstances of abuse it is *never* a child's fault.

We live in a violent society. One way that people cope with this reality is by convincing themselves that people who are brutally attacked, raped, or violated somehow "asked for it." People feel less vulnerable if they can blame victims of violence for their misfortune. Our society's tendency to fault victims increases the survivors' sense that the abuse was their fault and deepens their feelings of worthlessness and shame.

It is not just their experiences with their abusers which cause survivors to feel shameful but a profound belief that to their core they are ruined, worthless, and bad. Most victims suffer from painful low self-esteem. Many describe a sense of darkness inside, a void which fills the body and soul.

Considerable psychological theory and research has focused on the importance of self-esteem as a determinant of behavior and well-being. Researchers have linked high self-esteem to getting along well with others, to adaptive ways of coping with stress, and to creativity. A study conducted by the California Department of Mental Health (1979) found that positive self-esteem was the best predictor of higher health level. Self-esteem was a more significant predictor of health than physical environment, heredity, and availability of medical and psychological services.

Persons with low self-esteem tend to feel unloved and unlovable, isolated, unable to defend themselves, and afraid of angering others or drawing attention to themselves. Low self-esteem is consistently associated with depression, a frequent problem for the abused. Because many survivors were victimized when they were quite young and when their self-awareness and identity were still in formation, they may lack words to explain their profound sense of worthlessness. They may simply experience a pervasive, vague feeling of self-contempt.

A common cry of adult rape victims is, "I want my old self back and I can't find her." Because the emotional and physical devastation of the rape experience is so traumatic, the victim often finds her inner and outer world drastically changed. Because she has been defiled and overpowered in such a terrifying way, her entire understanding of who she is in relation to herself and the world is different. She even finds it difficult to remember who she was, what she felt like, and what the world seemed like before her rape. One woman divides her life into two eras: BR (before rape) and AR (after rape).

Many a survivor of childhood incestuous abuse can't remember a time before the abuse began. Consequently, she may have an even harder time finding herself. If her abuse began in early childhood, particularly before she could talk, she may have no sense of who she is apart from her victimization. Her experience of self may be confined to a shame-based identity which believes "I am a bad girl who deserves to have bad things done to me." Her unviolated, undistorted sense of I AM may have been so deeply hidden for so many years that she has no pre-incest memory of selfhood on which to draw.

One adult survivor of incest recalls,

> I don't remember when it all began nor even when it stopped. For many years I didn't even know what "it" was. But I knew I cried a lot, and I had always had a tense, difficult relationship with my father. I'd long struggled with depression and had attempted suicide numerous times to try and make the pain stop. I didn't have or know the words for incest or sexual abuse, but my heart and soul cried from their depths in pain until I could cry no more.
>
> Over the past twenty years, after many hours of group and individual therapy with some fourteen different professionals, and after reading abuse-related books and attending seminars on the subject, I have been able to slowly connect my disjointed symptoms and my jigsaw-like puzzle pieces along with stories and conversations and dreams. I have named the pain within—sexual abuse!

It is important for the adult victim of sexual abuse to learn to know, love, and heal the little child she used to be. Only then can she truly feel compassion for herself and open herself to healthy intimacy with others. As part of this process, one woman who had been abused wrote this poem to her abusive father.

**Lost and Found**

Little girl lost,
Who can count the cost?
Blond curls and eyes of blue,
Were never meant for someone as evil as you.
You took the innocence of a child,
But you're the one defiled!
I'm taking back my child and treating her with love.
She's being nurtured by me to be like her true Father above.
Her spirit survived and has come alive,
Hand in hand with Jesus, she will thrive.
Victory is mine; my goal to not be like you has been met,
My life will be full and happy, but that doesn't mean I'll forget.
Permanently scarred, my wounds are deep,
Yet I have an abiding peace and at last I can sleep.
    Signed,
    The Little Girl Found

## Body Issues

Sexual abuse is a devastating violation of the victim's body integrity. She has no control over the things which are done to her. Her freedom of choice about what she will do with her body is taken away. Her body is humiliated, hurt, and degraded. She is forced to participate in activities she doesn't understand. Her body is used for her abuser's pleasure with no regard for her feelings or her right to make decisions about her own body. In later years the body may have memories the mind can't recall. Body memories may flood the survivor at unexpected times as her body releases long-pent-up feelings of violation and pain.

Because her body was the means by which the victim experienced abuse, it is understandable that many a survivor feels great body-related conflict. "Of course I hate my body," one victim says. "It's what got me into trouble in the first place." It is no wonder that many victims of sexual abuse try to destroy their bodies, the vehicles of their pain, through suicide.

Even after the original abuse has ended, victims may revictimize their bodies through a variety of self-damaging behaviors. These often grow out of unconscious rage and hatred. While men are more likely to direct their rage and hatred toward others, women are more likely to direct it inward and to engage in self-damaging behaviors.

These behaviors may include self-neglect of health and personal hygiene; obesity; unnecessary risk-taking and argumentiveness which may provoke others to violent attack; addictive and compulsive behaviors; self-abusive relationships and sexual practices; self-mutilation through cutting, burning, hitting, and gouging the body; and suicidal thoughts and behaviors (Courtois, 1988).

Why would someone who has already been hurt so deeply want to keep hurting herself? Take self-mutilating behaviors such as cutting or burning oneself. It is important to remember that the unhealed inner pain resulting from sexual abuse is severe and unrelenting. The psychological pain is usually generalized, vague, and hard to define—a kind of free-floating terror in the victim's mind and spirit. By concentrating on a specific, external, localized pain caused by a burn or gash, the victim may find temporary relief from inner agony. The blood and wound become tangible externalizations of inner pain.

In addition, soon after the brain registers pain caused by a cut or burn, it releases endorphins. These are chemicals which act as a natural narcotic to lower the level of perceived pain.

One survivor explains her self-mutilating behaviors this way: "I felt like my body was filled with something dark and rotten. I thought if I cut myself, perhaps the putrid vileness would pour out and I would feel less evil. When I saw the jagged cut on my arm or leg, at least I knew why I hurt. And for a short time the pain did lessen."

In working with victims I have found that many isolate one part of their body to bear the hatred and disgust they feel for their entire body. One woman, who as a child had been forced to perform oral sex with her father, hated her mouth. She complained about its size and its shape. She owned dozens of tubes of lipstick with which she tried to disguise the "disgusting" natural color and shape of her lips. She usually held a hand over her mouth to hide it and thus made it hard for people to understand when she spoke.

Another woman blamed her full breasts, which had developed early in adolescence, for her father's abuse of her. For years she wore baggy, overly large clothes to disguise her breasts. "I really think I would be relieved to learn I had breast cancer and needed a double mastectomy."

Others express fear of the body, of its sensations and vulnerabilities. One strategy some victims develop to cope with these anxieties is to learn to dull physical sensations, to develop a generalized numbness in the body. "The pain to my little body was excruciating when he abused me. The only way I survived was to learn to turn off the feelings," says one survivor. "I wish I could feel good things in my body now, but I guess that's one more thing I've had to give up because of my abuse," she adds.

Those whose bodies responded pleasurably to stimulation during abuse often feel a deep sense of shame and betrayal. One survivor says, "I think I am most angry at myself, at my body, for responding sexually to the abuse. When my brother would come into my bed while I was sleeping, I would awaken and find my nipples erect and responsive to his stimulation. It was the ultimate sense of betrayal. To this day I don't feel I can trust my body and I hate it."

Even though an abused woman may intellectually understand that God has designed the human body to become aroused when touched in certain places and ways, she may have trouble forgiving her body. Insensitive therapists and clergy have compounded this dilemma by asking, "Now didn't you enjoy it just a little?" "Weren't you somewhat turned on by the experience?"

The implications of such questions have been tragically clear to the survivor. If her body responded physiologically to the abuse, she surely must have enjoyed it. Therefore, it must somehow have been her fault. Survivors and people who support them must be clear that blame resides with the adult who prematurely sexually aroused the child's body. Her body was simply responding in the way that God designed healthy bodies to react to touch and stimulation. It was not her or her body's fault. It was the fault of the abuser who chose to violate her body.

Disturbing body issues aren't confined just to victimized women. Many nonabused women, feeling they don't measure up to current cultural expectations of slenderness and beauty, develop disgust for their bodies. But because the survivor was abused through her body and often sees it as the cause of her pain, the relationship with her body becomes even more complicated than for the average nonabused woman. She becomes caught in a difficult double bind. Our culture says she must be pretty and sexually attractive to be of worth—yet she believes that by being pretty and sexually attractive she is vulnerable to further abuse.

One of the most dramatic and creative techniques devised by some victims to endure the pain and humiliation is to escape the body. Since they were usually unable physically to escape the abuse, they learned to escape mentally. The psychological term for this is "dissociation." It is also referred to as "splitting." As one victim says, "I was too little to stop the abuse and protect my body. But I was determined he wouldn't hurt the real me. So I learned how to float out of my body where he couldn't get me."

Victims tell of having had the sense of watching a movie or observing a play while their abuse was happening. Many report escaping by floating up to the ceiling or into a flower design on the wallpaper or to a safe corner of the room.

Some survivors find they still tend to "leave their bodies," often spontaneously, in times of stress or fear or during sexual activity. What was for the abused child an ingenious survival strategy may become a self-defeating pattern for the adult survivor. The escape strategy now makes it difficult for her to experience joyous physical intimacy and positive regard for her body self.

Because the body is seen as the enemy, survivors often express feelings of alienation, disgust, and shame about their bodies. It is not surprising that many develop serious problems as a result. The abused experience a high rate of eating disorders. Many girls abused as children develop anorexia when they enter puberty, wrongly thinking they will be safer from further abuse if they don't develop "sexy" bodies.

As one survivor says, "My abuse started when I was six. My dad would fondle me while he looked at magazine photos of voluptuous women. I was terrified of what might happen to me if I got big breasts. When I realized my body was developing, I basically stopped eating, thinking I could starve my breasts away."

Eating disorders such as anorexia, bulimia, and compulsive eating develop among some victims of abuse as they attempt to regain control over their bodies. No matter that the "control" obtained through the compulsive overeating and subsequent purging of bulimia, or the self-imposed starvation of anorexia, is dangerous and destructive. Victims often see such behaviors as the one means they have to exert authority over their power-stripped bodies.

Because of the vulnerable feelings associated with and attributed to her body, victims may try to hide their sexuality or femininity by carrying around excess weight, or by wearing baggy clothing or many layers which they believe may protect them.

"My compulsive eating wasn't only an attempt to fill the empty feeling inside me; it was also a way, I hoped, to make myself fat enough so that no man would ever again look at my body and lust after it. My obesity gave me a way to protect the scared little girl inside who was terrified of being abused again."

Friends and spouses are often baffled by a survivor's discomfort at wearing a bathing suit or undressing in situations which would be perfectly comfortable for others. One woman in her fifties still can't take a shower or bathe without wearing underclothes. "Every time I'm in the bathroom I get panicky that my brother will come in and start grabbing me and touching me again. I know this is crazy because he isn't even alive anymore!"

Every victim of childhood sexual abuse with whom I have worked in therapy has struggled with sexual problems of one sort or another. This is not surprising; for the victim sexual contact has become linked with powerlessness, pain, fear, anger, disgust, sadness, shame, and humiliation.

Sexuality problems for survivors tend to fall into two groups. Some abuse victims tend to respond to their childhood victimization by rejecting and fearing their sexuality. Other victims respond by becoming hypersexual and acting out in flagrantly sexual ways.

Victims who reject and fear their sexuality frequently report that as abused children they learned to leave their bodies or to go numb during sexual contact. When they become adults, this pattern obstructs joyous sexual relations. Other adult complaints include inhibited sexual desire, inability to experience orgasm, or pain during intercourse. Often the survivor and her partner have not made the connection between their sexual problems and her history of sexual abuse. When both partners are survivors of childhood sexual abuse, intimacy issues become even more complex.

Some survivors respond in a counterphobic way, becoming hypersexual. They may indiscriminately display their bodies, flaunt their sexuality in a compulsive manner, and turn sexually promiscuous. They may have concluded as abused children that sex was all they were good for and that sex equaled love. Their sense of self-worth and self-respect may have been stolen by the abuse, leaving them feeling damaged and defiled.

One survivor explains "By the time I left home at seventeen, I already felt like second-hand merchandise that nobody could ever respect or love. When Mom found out what had been going on with Dad, she started calling me a 'trashy whore,' and I guess I believed her."

Some victims have a sexualized identity which results from having concluded as children that they were only valued and loved for the sexual pleasure they could give others. This belief may continue into adulthood and lead to a pattern of sexual permissiveness and promiscuity. Because the primary attention and touch they received as children was abusive, adult survivors may likewise turn to promiscuous sex in their longing to be loved and touched.

Many of the one million women working in this country as prostitutes are victims of childhood sexual abuse (Herman, 1981). They may feel this occupation gives them a chance to do what they are good at and at least get paid for it. It may also confirm their belief that they are damaged property and not good for much besides being "trashy whores."

Untreated incest survivors often refer to themselves as bitches, witches, and whores. Violence, humiliation, pain, and shame are frequent components of the experience of sexual abuse. Because the victim has been programmed through early experiences to associate these with sexual arousal, prostitution may feel like a good fit for some survivors.

It is difficult for the survivor to believe her body is truly the "temple of the Holy Spirit" and that through creation she somehow embodies the image of God. James Nelson (1978) explains that the way we think and feel about our bodies will determine the way we think and feel about ourselves and others, the world, and God. For the victim of sexual abuse, the disrespectful use of her body indeed becomes the gateway for profound problems in many areas of her life.

## Relationship Issues

Another area of problems for the victim is in interpersonal relationships. Just as sexual abuse is a violent sin against the integrity and sanctity of the victim's body, so too is it a profound sin against her capacity to develop trusting, wholesome relationships. In an indirect way, any person who tries to develop an intimate relationship with someone abused as a child also becomes a victim of the original abuse.

Vital to any healthy intimate relationship is ability to trust. Sexual abuse destroys trust. It has been assumed by some that abuse by a stranger may be more traumatic than if the abuser is someone loved and trusted by the victim. The opposite, however, seems to be true.

Recovery from any sexual abuse is painful and difficult. When the abuser is known and trusted by the victim, additional issues arise. These issues are related to loss of confidence that there are people who can be trusted to have one's best interests at heart and keep one safe. If a child can't trust her own family members to treat her with respect and integrity, who can she trust? No one, is the sad conclusion reached by many victims. Survivors often feel betrayed by both the abuser and the nonoffending family members for not keeping them safe. This sense of betrayal impacts the victims' ability to form other healthy, trusting relationships.

Because they have been hurt by people they trusted and loved, victims may develop deep suspicion and cynicism toward intentions and behaviors of others. They may have difficulty evaluating people's motivations realistically and objectively. Given these struggles, it is understandably hard for unhealed victims to develop healthy relationships.

Intense emotional confusion arises when the victim is simultaneously being abused (be it sexually, emotionally, or physically) and being told by the abuser that she is loved. A distorted understanding of "love" results. "I decided when I was about ten years old that if people who love you treat you the way my father did," says one survivor, "then I didn't need and didn't want anybody else ever to love me again."

The disturbing combination of love and abuse, of trust and violence, causes in some victims a profound disturbance of ability to form healthy relationships. Some victims vow they will never again get close emotionally to anyone who might once more abuse and misuse them. The impression such people may give is that they are hard, emotionally cold, and aloof. These behaviors often mask a profound inner loneliness and a sense of pain and vulnerability.

The confusion which results when a child is abused by someone she trusts leads some survivors into patterns of repeated victimization. They may believe that to get love they must be willing to put up with abusive behavior. As a therapist I am often amazed at victims' ability to endure dysfunctional, abusive relationships in adulthood. I am likewise grieved by many victims' difficulty in saying and believing, "I didn't deserve to be abused then, and I don't deserve to be abused now!"

Many victims are confused and saddened by their ability to become involved in one abusive relationship after another. "I consciously set out to find a husband who was the opposite of my father," says one victim. "Even though their looks and personalities and interests are very different, my husband treats me in ways very similar to how Dad treated me."

Another woman told me, "I've been married four times. Each

time I was sure this one was different from any man I'd loved before. But wouldn't you know, they all ended up treating me in the same abusive, controlling way in which my father did. No matter how different they look and act, deep down inside, every man I've ever loved turns out to be just like my father."

## Faith and Spirituality Issues

The process of healing is even more complex and difficult for victims abused in religious settings (such as church schools, religious homes, or churches) by persons who represented spiritual authority or articulated religious faith.

A survivor says, "It is confusing and destructive when your abuse and your religious instruction come from the same person." Another survivor puts it this way, "It is very hard to have a healthy spiritual foundation when sexual violation and teachings about God came to me from the same person."

One woman comments, "Each Sunday I'd go to church with my family and hear God loved and was watching over me. Then we'd go home and I'd get abused again and wonder why God didn't protect me from these people who went to church. In my family it was not acceptable to sew on Sundays but it was acceptable to abuse children. Talk about crazy-making stuff!"

In my research with survivors victimized by religious persons, many report great adult discomfort and pain when they sit in church. For some it brings back memories of ineffectual childhood attempts to let people in their congregations know what was happening to them so that someone would intervene and stop the abuse. Some express overwhelming feelings of having their trust in these good people betrayed by their insensitivity and blindness to the abuse.

For others, being in church activates painful memories of sitting with the family on Sunday mornings, *appearing* to be a fine Christian family, while abusive, terrifying things were happening in the family during the week. While the precise reasons may vary, many survivors of abuse report being unable truly to worship in congregational settings.

For survivors whose sexual abuse was committed by people

involved in ritualistic, occultic practices, communion becomes a frightening event. The symbolic connection between the wine and the blood of Jesus becomes terrifying for one forced to drink human blood as part of ritualistic abuse. One adult survivor of ritualistic abuse was able to participate in communion only after being put into a light trance, visualizing the individual stages of the communion service, and asking Jesus to be present at each step of the service. Another woman, who has no conscious recollection of her abuse having had ritualistic components, says, "I can't participate in communion without afterwards crying deeply, in much the same way that I cry after sexual intimacy."

Not surprisingly, research has found that women who were incestuously abused as children have a significantly higher rate of defection from their childhood religion than women who weren't abused. Russell (1983) reports that 53 percent of the women in her study of incest victims had rejected their childhood religion. Apparently the multifaceted disillusionment of having been abused affects ability to embrace the religion of the abuser.

When the victimization occurs in a nonreligious system, the survivor may be able to label the experience and the offender as sinful and evil. She may in later life turn to God and the church and experience grace and joy as she matures spiritually. She may wish she had had her current spiritual insights and resources earlier and may assume that if she had, they would have somehow protected her from the abuse.

Profound spiritual damage occurs, however, when the abuser and victim are religious people. If the victim called out to God for protection during her time of abuse, yet the abuse continued, she may subsequently view God as uncaring. She may see God as aloof, disinterested in both the human condition and her personal well-being, impotent to intervene in human matters.

When asked about the impact of her childhood abuse by a "very religious father" on her adult spirituality, one woman said,

> As an abused little girl, I prayed and read my Bible both morning and night, and put half of my allowance in the church offering every week, and promised God I'd become a missionary and do any-

thing he asked me to do if he'd just stop my daddy from coming into my room at night. When God didn't answer my prayers, I decided either there wasn't a God or that he was mean and not interested in what happens to little girls. I decided I didn't like God and didn't need a God like him.

Many survivors report having felt abandoned by God. "Where was God when I was being abused?" survivors often ask. Many see God as unfair and unfaithful. They hold God responsible for their abuse. Others, uncomfortable with such conclusions, decide God isn't the problem—they are. If an all-powerful God allows bad things to happen, it must be punishment they deserve for being bad.

This flawed image of the self combined with a distorted image of God makes it difficult to feel God's unconditional love. Many survivors are devout in their practice of spiritual disciplines yet struggle to experience a sense of personal relationship with God. Sadly, they once more conclude that the problem is theirs instead of the result of having been abused and violated.

Victims often tell of a love-hate relationship with the Bible. They find comfort in passages which tell of biblical characters' struggle with pain and abandonment; they find hope in reading of Jesus' loving treatment of the downtrodden and powerless. But many survivors remember that the Bible was used to coerce them into abusive submission or feeling they were responsible for the abuse. The Scriptures used most often by an abuser seem to be the commandment "honor your father and your mother, so that your days may be long in the land that the Lord your God is giving you" (Exod. 20:12) and "children, obey your parents" (Eph. 6: 1).

In many Christian circles, the human father is seen as the ultimate authority next to God. As one victim of incestuous abuse told me, "Now it doesn't make sense to me, but as a child I had the feeling that by saying no to my father I was really saying no to and rejecting God." Another woman had recurring flashbacks of childhood abuse in which it seemed to her she was having sex with God. She was shocked, disgusted, and baffled by these images until she recalled her childhood confusion between her very powerful (and abusive) father and God.

Some victims from Christian homes tell of being simultaneously abused and having Scriptures quoted to them. One woman says,

> As my father abused me, he quoted Bible verses to show how bad I was—primarily verses from 1 John. He said I was going to hell because I didn't love him. Perfect love casts out fear. If I was afraid it meant I didn't have love. God would never love me because I didn't love my dad. I would tell him I did love him and would do whatever he asked except that sexual stuff but he would again work it around that I was sinning. In the last days before Christ returns, there will be children with 'inordinate' (not the usual) affection for their parents. I was one of this last generation's terrible sinners.

This woman's father was an active layman in his congregation. He taught Sunday school, led the weekly church prayer meetings, and conducted daily family devotions. Not surprisingly, his daughter has suffered intense spiritual and emotional confusion and pain in her adult years.

A child's interaction with parents and other significant people is crucial to the development of an appropriate understanding of God. When parents and others are insensitive to a child's feelings and treat the child in selfish, abusive, disrespectful ways, the child's concept of God becomes distorted.

Because most sexual offenders are male, the dominant image used in Christian churches of God the Father becomes problematic for many women abused by their earthly fathers. One survivor says, "It has been hard for me to trust and love the heavenly Father when I can only feel fear and distrust and disgust for my earthly father because of all the years he violated and abused my body and spirit." Another woman confesses, "Whenever someone refers to God the Father, I visualize a man with a huge, violent penis like the one my dad used to rape me as a little girl."

Before ending this chapter, I must pay homage to the strength of many survivors. While the scars of childhood victimization are lifelong, many have found the safety, support, and resources to be healed. Many survivors are awesome tributes to God's healing power and grace. Charlene Epp writes of her victory over incest.

i am overcoming the darkness of my experience with incest
i can claim victory
God has been there like the steady beat of a drum
even when I was in the depths of the dark night of my soul
    in the deep abyss
God was present with me
though the dark surrounded me
    seemed to envelop me
yet God was there
i was not aware of God's presence
    i could not name it
but it's as if i were connected by an umbilical cord to God during
        this time
    receiving the sustenance to endure the darkness

though i cannot name your shape God
    you were there providing me strength
and gradually you have revealed your Presence in the form of
        light
    Light that dispels fear of the darkness
    Light that gives and renews Life    Energy    and Vitality
for i see that though the umbilical cord has been cut
    my lifeline to you has not been severed
you are present in many forms
    it is only i who can limit my access to you

even if i walk again into shadows and darkness
    your Presence will reach to me there
    in the warm clear Liquid that fills and gives me color
    in the gentle firm hand clasp of a Friend walking beside me
and because i know and am assured of your Presence
    i know you will cast off the shadows and darkness on other's
        lives
    and they too will claim the Light
it is in this way that you remain Sovereign
    in the revelation of your gentle firm inviting Presence

your Strength oh God is deceptive
it appears weak in the eyes of the world
but it is a strength that endures eternity
just as marathon runners save their strength to endure the long
        distance

and pace themselves at a steady rate
so you are oh God
Paced as a runner
Steady as the beat of the drum
my victory is that i recognize you and your Presence in my life

Another survivor, Elizabeth Gingrich, can today affirm God's healing touch on her life. She says, "It seems that healing and wholeness have been my pull and direction over the years—even before I consciously knew what needed healing." She wrote the following to reflect this movement in her life.

struggling and surviving
crying and praying
weeping and despairing
talking and writing and writing and writing
waiting and wading
through the darkness and pain
is leading to more and more light
to more and more grace
and to more and more healing.

Those who have survived and done the painful work of recovery are often people with an astounding core of inner vitality and strength. Being around those who are healing and who have found a creative channel for their inner energy is a moving experience. Survivors who have walked through the valley of the shadow of death and come through to the light are a powerful testimony to the resilience and strength of the human spirit. They are a walking tribute to the power of divine healing.

The difficult inner work of remembering and healing which such survivors have done is not just for themselves but also for the generations which follow. They are a joy and inspiration to behold. Instead of shunning them and wishing they'd go away with their terrible tales, we need to honor their strength, salute their courage, and learn from their journey.

## Chapter 3

# Denial, Incidence, and Factors Related to Abuse

## Denial

Individuals and institutions alike use denial as a way to avoid the pain of something which causes distress and anxiety. When we don't want to or are unable to face a disturbing reality, we use denial to pretend that the disturbing event didn't really happen. As was discussed in chapter 2, victims of sexual abuse often use denial as a way of trying to protect themselves against the terrifying reality of their vulnerability and abuse. When victims feel safe enough, they may stop denying their abusive past and begin remembering and recovering.

Institutions such as churches are also capable of profound denial. Institutional denial of the reality of sexual abuse has compounded the pain for victims, who often feel crazy when they are told their reality is not possible among "our kind of people, not among Christians." Individual and institutional denial have made it difficult to understand the extent and causes of sexual abuse. Something denied can not be examined, understood, or prevented.

Many professionals believe sexual abuse of children by a relative is the most under reported of all crimes. No other offense is so effectively shrouded in secrecy. Most victims never tell anyone, and their abuse remains a proverbial skeleton in the family closet. Russell's (1983) landmark study found that only 2 percent of women who had been sexually abused as children reported it.

Beyond the intimidating threats and bribes for silence made by abusers, many children sense their accusations would cause severe family disruption. In addition to fear that the abuser will be removed from the home and even sent to prison, children suspect that their public accusation will result in family stigmatization and ostracism. Some victims and family members fear loss of financial support should the abusive parent be removed from the home. Others fear the emotional turmoil that will occur in the family if the abuse is reported. Many victims sense they will be blamed for both the abuse and the resultant family disruption.

The discomfort of the church in speaking of things sexual surely makes it difficult for a sexually abused child to approach church people. Fear of congregational responses also makes it unlikely that the abusive family will turn to the congregation for help. A young victim told her mother about sexual abuse by her father which had been occurring for many years. The mother's first response was, "Well, I certainly hope you haven't told anyone else about this—especially not anyone from church—because if you have, we can never step inside that church again!"

Many victims, particularly children of pastors or other community or church leaders, know accusations of abuse would be hard for most people to believe. As one victim of a prominent church-leader father says, "Who would have believed me if I had told them the things my highly visible and respected father was doing to me? I was just a little girl; he was a famous man in our denomination. It would have been my word against his, and I knew who people would believe."

The psychotherapeutic community, which knows the profound damage resulting from sexual abuse, might be expected to work hard to develop an atmosphere encouraging victims to recognize and disclose abuse. Regrettably, this has not been the case. Until recently, the professional community has not made the problem of sexual abuse a priority.

One reason for professional avoidance and denial regarding sexual abuse of children may be related to the ideological foundations of psychotherapy. Sigmund Freud, demigod of modern psychology, perpetuated the view that when clients reported abuse by their fathers, these incidents were usually fantasies rather than real events.

Originally Freud took a different position. Based on his case studies, he concluded that incest was not rare and confined to the poor and mentally retarded as was then commonly maintained. In his 1896 paper "The Etiology of Hysteria," Freud argued that at the core of every case of hysteria was childhood sexual trauma caused by parents. But Freud was never comfortable with this hypothesis because of what it inferred about respectable men.

This theory provoked a storm of protest from professionals and laypeople. Social pressure seems to have persuaded Freud to change his theory from childhood sexual trauma to oedipal fantasies. Sexual abuse of children is repugnant to most people. It may evoke subconscious fears of one's own potential for abuse or victimization. It is less threatening and disturbing to assume that stories of childhood abuse are fabrications and fantasies, as is the notion that women who are raped somehow wanted or asked for it.

Florence Rush, Judith Herman, and Jeffrey Masson have provided disturbing insights into another factor involved in Freud's unwillingness to maintain his original theory. They believe Freud was disturbed by his own sexual fantasies toward his daughter and was relieved to alter his original position (Russell, 1986).

Freud's subsequent focus on the sexual interests of children tended to blame the child's seductiveness and not the adult's irresponsibility (Finkelhor, 1984). Freud's legacy to the field of psychotherapy in the area of sexual abuse of children has been a strong and lasting bias that most childhood stories of abuse are not based on reality and, if true, are related to the child's seductiveness.

Although this may change, now that abuse is receiving more attention, training programs for psychotherapists reflect Freud's bias, as seen in the minimal attention given to sexual abuse. A survey in New Mexico illustrates. Names were chosen randomly from a telephone directory under the listings of "Marriage, Family, Child, and Individual Counselors" and "Psychologists." Only therapists with graduate degree designations were included in the sample. Each psychotherapist was asked, "In your professional academic or practicum training program, did you receive any training in working with victims of sexual abuse?"

Of the respondents, less than 4 percent said they had received training in this area. Several noted that while in their internship or practicum, they had female clients allude to having been sexually abused by their fathers. The therapists-in-training had gone to their supervisors for consultation on how to proceed. Two supervisors suggested the women were probably making up the stories to get sympathy or manipulate the therapist. A third supervisor told the intern not to let the client "get bogged down with past history" but to keep her "moving along toward what's important in her life now."

This lack of openness and training in dealing with victims of sexual abuse is not unique to New Mexico practitioners. Judith Herman (1981) says,

> The tradition of institutional denial has resulted in a situation in which supervisors are no more knowledgeable than beginners. Until recently there was no body of professional literature to offer the therapist intellectual support. There was no body of practical experience transmitted by oral tradition other than the continuing tradition that questions the veracity of patients' complaints (p. 180).

## Incidence

Incest is strictly forbidden in most cultures. Strong taboos against incest have meant that responses of either denial or shock and horror are typical when incest is reported. Despite almost universal regulations against incest, researchers have found evidence that it has been widespread since biblical times. While the true extent of incestuous abuse will never be known, evidence reveals a longstanding pattern of *overt public prohibition* and outcry against incest joined with *covert acceptance* in most cultures (Courtois, 1988). Victims are thus caught in a double bind—they are unable to share their stories of victimization and cannot get outside validation for their experiences.

Current statistics on sexual abuse are astounding. Research indicates that at least one third of all American women were sexually abused before age eighteen (Blume, 1990). In an analysis of previous research studies done on sexual abuse, Finkelhor (1986) found reported rates which ranged from 6 percent to 62 percent for females and from 3 percent to 31 percent for males. The lowest rates indicate that sexual abuse of children is significant. The higher rates indicate an epidemic. It is no longer possible to ignore the pervasiveness of this problem in our society.

It is disturbing to realize that what cannot be remembered cannot be reported. Many professionals suspect that, in North America, the actual number of women sexually abused during childhood may be over half the population. Sexual abuse can no longer be considered an isolated tragedy which befalls a few unfortunate individual children. It is instead an epidemic affecting us all.

The true extent of sexual abuse will never be known. Beyond the general reluctance to report abuse, many incidents are repressed and unavailable to conscious memory throughout much—and often all—of a victim's life. If the abuse occurred before the child had words to name or understand what was happening, it is particularly likely that the abuse will be forgotten by the logical, language-oriented part of the brain. The sensations and emotions associated with abuse are "remembered" by the body. But if asked, many adults who were sexually abused as young children sincerely do not recall the abuse and declare they are not abuse victims.

## Related Factors

Abuse in general has been considered more prevalent among poorer, less educated families. Research has indeed found a strong relationship between lower social class and physical abuse (Pelton, 1981). The added frustrations which often accompany poverty (joblessness, inadequate housing, lack of education, hopelessness, and despair) may indeed contribute to an increase in violence and physical aggression.

But the relationship between *sexual* abuse and socioeconomic level appears to be a different story. Most researchers have not found a significant relationship between social class of the victim's family and incidence of sexual abuse. For example, Peters' 1984 study of Los Angeles women found no relationship between sexual abuse and either parental level of education or social class.

Russell's 1986 study also failed to find a relationship between sexual abuse and the father's occupational and educational level. While the child welfare system makes it easier to identify abuse among the poor, most current research finds that sexual abuse and social class are unrelated. The problem is widespread among all socioeconomic levels.

Very little has been done to examine ethnic differences in the occurrence of sexual abuse. Studies which have looked at ethnicity and have controlled for city size and other demographic factors have not found differences in rates of abuse among African-American and Anglo populations (Finkelhor, 1986). Russell (1986) and others have found slightly higher rates of sexual abuse among Latino women and lower rates among Asian and Jewish women. When women of a particular ethnic group report a low incidence of abuse, does this reflect a less abusive culture or higher reluctance to talk about sexual matters with a researcher? Ethnicity and sexual abuse is a relationship needing further study.

A common perception is that the social isolation of rural living increases the risk of being sexually abused. While social isolation has been correlated with other forms of child abuse and neglect, no consistent evidence that sexual abuse is more common in rural than urban areas has been found (Garbarino and Stocking, 1980).

Numerous studies have, however, identified another aspect of social isolation which does appear related to abuse—sexual abuse victims tend to be isolated from their peers. Finkelhor (1984) found a higher incidence of sexual abuse among women who at age twelve had two or fewer friends. Fromuth (1983) and Peters (1984) also confirmed this finding. Finkelhor hypothesized that if children have few friends, they may feel a need for contact and friendship on which sexual predators capitalize.

Another explanation for this correlation may be that social isolation is less a risk factor and more a result of victimization. Abused children often feel deep shame and stigmatization. They assume erroneously that what happened to them is unique. Many victims think that people can tell by looking at them that something terrible and shameful has happened to them. Consequently, abuse victims may socially isolate themselves.

Several sociological factors related to parents and family have been found to have a strong connection to abuse. An increasing number of studies have identified various forms of parental absence as highly correlated with sexual abuse. Finkelhor (1984) found that having lived apart from a natural mother resulted in an almost threefold higher risk for abuse. Finkelhor, Fromuth, and Peters all found that girls who had ever lived without natural fathers were at higher risk of being sexually abused (in Finkelhor, 1986).

Living with a disabled or ill mother has also been associated with a greater likelihood of abuse. Peters (1984), Finkelhor (1984) and Herman and Hirschman (1981) found higher rates of sexual victimization among girls with mothers who were frequently ill (most commonly due to alcoholism, depression, or psychosis) and who were exhausted from many children and pregnancies.

A revealing finding related to parental relationships has surfaced in a substantial number of studies (Landis, 1956; Finkelhor, 1984; Peters, 1984; P. Miller, 1976). Victims report distant emotional relationships with their mothers and are less likely to name their mothers as their primary source of sex information.

Abused daughters tend to see their mothers as having less power and authority in the home than their fathers. Other studies have reported that victims received little affection from either their mothers or fathers and reported having poorer relationships with their parents than did the nonabused population (Finkelhor, 1986).

Victims of sexual abuse often report poor relationships between their parents. Some researchers (Finkelhor 1984; Fromuth, 1983; Peters, 1984) found higher rates of abuse among women who reported that their parents either had unhappy marriages or showed little marital affection. It cannot, however, be concluded from such data that marital stress or alienation causes sexual abuse.

Another sociological factor emerges as a risk factor for sexual abuse—presence in the home of a non-biologically-related father. Russell's (1986) large-scale study of incestuously abused girls found that women raised by both their biological or adoptive parents were the least likely to be sexually abused (15 percent in this study). Among women raised by biological mothers only, the incidence of incestuous abuse was 18 percent. However, 28 percent of the women raised by a stepfather and a biological mother reported incestuous abuse.

Several factors may explain the increased risk of those raised by a stepfather. Traditional cultural taboos against sexual contact between stepfathers and stepdaughters are milder and thus possibly easier to violate than those forbidding father-daughter contact. Early child-parent bonding and dependency among stepchildren and stepfather is usually lacking. Stepfathers who haven't experienced this nurturing process may more easily see the stepchild as a possible sexual partner (Finkelhor, 1986).

Finkelhor (1986) found that girls with stepfathers were sexually abused at a higher rate by other men also. He suggests that dating mothers may bring home sexually exploitative men who take advantage of daughters. They may also bring into the family other step-relatives who feel fewer cultural restraints about being sexually involved with the daughters. Stepfathers may also be less protective than a biological father when others become sexually aggressive toward their stepdaughters.

# Philosophical and Theological Factors

Some factors related to sexual abuse are philosophical and theological. There are beliefs about the human body and sexuality which predate Christianity but which still exert strong influence on Christians. To fully understand sexual abuse, it is helpful to explore some of these factors.

Knowing how to live with integrity as people both spiritual and sexual is not a new dilemma. The uneasiness with which human embodiment and sexuality are regarded is not a modern problem. Its old, deep roots predate Christianity. The Old Testament, however, reflects from its very beginning the belief that sexuality is a good gift from God. At the dawn of history, as Genesis records it, the first human words are the erotic love poem, "This at last is bone of my bone and flesh of my flesh" (Genesis 2:23). In the next verse of the Genesis story, the man and woman move toward each other to become one flesh, naked and unashamed.

Subsequent stories in the Old Testament treat human sexuality as a good and natural part of life. Explicit stories of sexual relations are told. Most accounts suggest that the main purpose for marriage and sexuality is to produce children. But sexuality is also portrayed as the vehicle for romantic passion. Although later Christians preferred to read it as an allegory of spiritual longing, Song of Songs is graphic, erotic poetry that celebrates physical beauty and passionate sexual love.

The ancient Hebrews sometimes used the verb "to know" as a synonym for sexual intercourse, thus combining knowing and desiring as an expression of sexual communion at its best. The psalmist at times reflects a sensual component to the human longing for desiring and knowing God, consistent with the Old Testament view of the unity of mind, body, and spirit. For example, Psalm 42:1-2 says, "As a deer longs for flowing streams, so my soul longs for you, O God. My soul thirsts for God, for the living God. When shall I come and behold the face of God?"

But body-denying influences gradually affected the Hebrews. These influences may have come from such lands as Persia, where salvation was correlated with sexual restriction. Sexist dualism (the subordination of women) is both a major root and an expression of this sexual alienation (Nelson, 1978). Men regarded themselves as superior in matters of the mind and soul and took responsibility for leading in those areas of communal life. Women became identified with emotions, sensuality, and the body. Monthly restrictions and complicated rituals associated with purification after menstruation regularly and powerfully indoctrinated both males and females with the belief that women's bodies were unclean. Therefore, women were considered inferior to men.

Pagan Greek and Roman beliefs subsequently influenced Christianity's understanding of the human body and sexuality. Greek dualism divided the universe into opposing dimensions—the spiritual and the material realms. Humans were thought to have a soul and a body—a higher and a lower nature. The body was a prison of the soul, which was in constant battle against temptations and weaknesses of the flesh. The human task was to tame the body and its desires so the soul could escape bodily corruption.

Plato ( 427-347 B.C.) was an articulate and influential spokesperson for this dualistic view of humans. He used the terms "idea" and "matter" to designate two opposing universal principles. Ideas were eternal, invisible, absolute, without beginning or end. Matter, the material world of objects experienced with the five senses, was an imperfect imitation of ideas. Christianity was influenced by the platonic idea that the immaterial soul was superior to and in conflict with the human body.

Other pagan Greek philosophers also influenced the intellectual climate in which Christianity developed. Philosophers who were ascetics assumed that true virtue depends on abstinence from sexual activity. Democritus conceptualized virtue as the exercise of intelligence. Since sexual activity was distracting to the pursuits of the mind, he discouraged engaging in sexual relations. The Stoic Musonius Rufus claimed that marital intercourse was permissible only for procreation. He taught that sexual activity for pleasure, even in the marital relationship, was disgusting (Bullough and Bullough, 1977).

Philo, an Alexandrian Jew born at the end of the first century B.C., was particularly influential on later Christian writers. Philo took the Jewish teaching of the need to multiply and replenish the earth and combined it with the Greek and Roman tradition that sexual intercourse could only be justified for procreative purposes. He compared spouses who had intercourse without intending procreation to pigs or goats. He also taught that the original sin of Adam and Eve was sexual desire.

It was in this cultural, philosophical milieu that Christianity developed. These ascetic, dualistic ideas are not predominant in the New Testament, but later Christians were influenced by these writers.

Jesus had relatively little to say about sexuality and marriage. When he did talk about sex, he generally stayed within the Old Testament tradition. This is not to say that human sexuality was not important to him, but rather that sexual concerns were subordinate to his broader concern of proclaiming the coming kingdom of God. What Jesus did say is striking in contrast to the accepted practices and attitudes of his day. Jesus condemned infidelity and divorce as violations of God's intentions for the union of woman and man. His consistent concern for the oppressed was consistent with his rejection of divorce; when disposed of by male decree, women were treated as property.

Likewise, Jesus was not satisfied with legalistic, superficial faithfulness in marriage. He called for faithfulness and purity of the heart. In Matthew 5:27-28 Jesus said that one who even lusted after another was an adulterer. Jesus was not condemning all sexual desires or fantasies. "Lust" in New Testament Greek is a word which is broadly used and whose meaning depends on the context. It can be translated to mean "strongly desire."

In these verses Jesus seems to be condemning sinful lust, lust which becomes a fixation, an ongoing drive fueled by allowing the mind to play around with fantasies of sexual involvement with someone other than the marriage partner. This is different than a fleeting physiological or emotional response to an aesthetically pleasing person.

Singleness was affirmed in the New Testament as a valid choice for believers. Some texts speak to the preferability of singleness, not because it allowed avoiding sexual relations, but because it freed persons more fully to invest in kingdom work.

Marriage among believers was also affirmed in the New Testament. In Ephesians 5:21-23, Paul compared the husband/wife relationship to the union between Christ and the church. The key elements in both covenants are love and faithfulness. Paul elevated the sexual union in marriage beyond being merely a pleasurable physical act to one which engaged the whole person in ways which expressed commitment and self-disclosure (Nelson, 1978). Both Jesus and Paul, however, avoided affirming marriage and sexuality as the highest good—giving primacy instead to the kingdom of God.

Gnostic interpreters of Christianity believed the soul was a spark of the divine imprisoned in the human body. Salvation consisted of escaping bodily defilement by abstaining from sexual relations and living an ascetic life. Although church leaders condemned the Gnostics as heretics, the church was influenced by some of their teachings and practices. At times the early Christian communities seemed to have tried to gain status and converts by outdoing the Gnostics at ascetic practices and sexual abstinence.

By the end of the second century, Gnostic influence had diminished. Nevertheless, the church retained a strong discomfort with and hostility toward sexuality. The combination of Greco-Roman philosophy and Gnostic beliefs made sexuality a matter of great tension from the second to the fifth century. As part of creation which God had made and pronounced good, the human body, sexuality, and marriage had to be good. Yet sexual desire was a powerful drive seemingly in conflict with spiritual holiness. From the male point of view, women were responsible for inciting sensual passions. The best way to take away the power of sex was to promote celibacy. Virginity and sexual abstinence were held up as the "higher religious way" (Carmody, 1979).

There were many instances of the glorification of celibacy and deprecation of marital intercourse. Origen and other early Christians drew praise for castrating themselves in an attempt to increase their efficacy in prayer (Carmody, 1979). Tertullian taught that losing one's chastity was worse than losing one's life. He did resist what appears to be explicitly an inclination to condemn intercourse in marriage but seemed perplexed as to why it was ever allowed by God.

More than other early church leaders, Clement of Alexandria defended the dignity of marriage. But his preference for the unmarried state was strong. Marriage was intended only for procreation. Conception should be accomplished with as little emotion as possible. He taught that married men did well to practice abstinence and believed heaven would finally free both men and women from sexuality.

In the third century, there was a marked increase in clerical pressure to be celibate. John Chrysostom, an influential church leader in the East, taught that since the world was already populated, marriage and sexual relations were a concession to sinful desires.

Augustine was the most influential teacher of the early Western church on issues of marriage and human sexuality. His concern was primarily with the genital aspects of human sexuality. The original sin, he believed, was transmitted through the inherently sinful character of sexual libido. Augustine saw a clear connection between the fall and "concupiscence" (sexual desire). He believed that every sexual act was directly related to original sin, binding the participants more firmly to the fall. This belief that Adam's guilt was sexually transmitted from generation to generation through sexual intercourse had been a Greek precept for many years before Augustine's time.

It was a logical step from this premise to Augustine's belief that sexual intercourse was the greatest threat to spirituality. For Augustine, sexual pleasure in marriage was a venial or pardonable sin. If procreation was not possible (as after menopause), it was a mortal sin. Therefore a man should love his wife's soul, but hate her body as an enemy. Virginity was elevated as the preferred state for Christians. For those unable to maintain this lifestyle, marriage was reluctantly permitted (Ruether, 1974).

Throughout the Middle Ages, theologians and church leaders considered marriage ethically inferior to celibacy. The biological consequences of marriage (loss of virginity and bearing of children) were, in the medieval perspective, symbols and painful reminders of woman's fallen nature. This low view of marriage and the new piety of the eleventh and twelfth centuries brought increasing numbers of men and women to monastic, celibate orders.

The Reformation movement of the 1500s brought changes to the church's view of marriage. Through private Bible study, Martin Luther found the Catholic Church's apologetic view of marriage unbiblical. He denounced the elevated status of celibacy and said marriage must not be seen as ethically inferior.

Luther not only affirmed marriage as a good gift of God but elevated it above all other states. He considered marriage the "good and normal" way of life and saw the family as a school of faith in which people could practice a life of loving service as in no other living arrangement. Rejecting his earlier vow of celibacy, Luther married Katy, a former nun. Together they raised nine children (Hargrove, 1983).

While Luther by example and teaching challenged many medieval beliefs about celibacy and marriage, he apparently had ambivalent feelings about sexuality. Like Augustine, Luther thought intercourse could never occur without sin. In his 1522 treatise on marriage, Luther examined the biblical foundations for a positive theology of marriage and affirmed that sexuality and procreation are part of a "divine ordinance." But Luther's treatise on "The Estate of Marriage" ended by saying, "Intercourse is never without sin; but God excuses it by his grace because the estate of marriage is his work, and he preserves in and through the sin all that good which he has implanted and blessed in marriage." This negative view of sexual relations was also reflected in Luther's 1535-1536 lectures on Genesis, where numerous times he referred to sexual desire and marital relations as occasions of "shame" and "disgust."

Luther's paradoxical view that marriage and procreation are part of God's divine plan, yet sexual relations are sinful and shameful, is one more component of the theological and philosophical inheritance of the contemporary church. This legacy reflects and contributes to the ongoing uneasiness among Christians with the human body and its sexual urges.

The long-standing discomfort and suspicion with which the church has regarded the human body and sexuality are significant factors in the occurrence of sexual abuse among Christians. Suspicion of sexuality contributes to the shroud of silence and secrecy which surround abuse.

Because human sexuality has long been considered in opposition to human spirituality (the "appropriate" arena of concern for the church), there has been a lack of sensitive teaching regarding the place of healthy sexuality in the Christian life. Rules and pronouncements have been given in an attempt to help Christians control their sexual passions. There have been vehement teachings on the evils of unbridled lust and warnings about the dangers of the flesh. The result too often has been to perpetuate the belief that sexuality is evil, dangerous, to be feared and hated by those on a spiritual quest.

When something is feared and loathed, it becomes hard to face openly and easy to repress. When Christians struggle with sexual temptations, the church is rarely experienced as a safe, appropriate place to disclose weakness and seek counsel and support. Instead, the tendency has been to deny and repress uncomfortable, inappropriate sexual longings and to pretend to ourselves and others in the church that they don't exist. Rarely are sexual urges shared in a Christian setting in an attempt to gain a framework of accountability and support for working out a healthy sexual life. But the more people try to suppress and deny sexual urges, the more powerful they become; those powerful sexual urges are more likely to break through the wall of repression in unhealthy, destructive, and abusive ways.

Because we rarely talk about healthy sexuality in the church, how do those struggling with unhealthy sexual temptations and urges bring them to the congregation? It is critical that the church develop a holistic, biblical understanding of the human body and sexuality.

The church must provide an atmosphere in which members can claim and share this powerful part of themselves. Denominations and congregations must work to develop, explain, and then live out in practical ways a healthy theology of the body and human sexuality. Chapter 11 will explore practical ways congregations can move in this direction.

## Chapter 4

# The Perpetrator

## A Perpetrator's Story

This story was shared with me by a perpetrator of sexual abuse.

> I was raised in a large Christian family. Church services and activities were the focus of our family life even more than the farm chores we all had to help with. We went to church twice on Sundays and every Wednesday night. My father was an elder in our church all the years I can remember. He was a stern, rigid man and had very strict rules.
>
> Whenever we violated his rules, we were whipped with willow branches he kept both in the kitchen and out in the barn. I remember once my mother crying and telling him that we were "just kids being kids" and didn't deserve to be beaten. He grabbed her by the collar and asked if she was defying him. He told her if she interfered in his attempts to raise God-fearing children, she'd be the next one "to get it." I don't remember my mom ever again publicly disagreeing with him or sticking up for us, but I do remember her crying a lot.
>
> Neither of my parents ever talked to me about sex. Because we lived on a farm, I figured things out for myself. When I got to school some of the older boys told me how "people do it." When I

started having sexual feelings myself, it was confusing and frightening. I wasn't sure what was happening to me but was afraid to talk to anyone about it.

At a high school church camp, I heard a sermon about masturbation, although the word was never used. The speaker explained why it was a terrible sin, but now I can't remember what the reasons were. At the time they made a lot of sense. The more I tried not to do it, the more I wanted to do it. I was sure my pimples were caused by my hidden sin, which could no longer be hidden since it was now broadcast all over my face.

After high school I attended Bible school for one year. There I met the woman I married. From the beginning it was a difficult relationship. That was partly, I suppose, because she was so different from my mother. My wife has a big mouth and a strong will. When I tried being a man and husband like I learned from my dad, she got real pushy and told me she wouldn't put up with it.

Our children came along real fast and that made things even more tense between us. Every time I'd try to discipline the children she'd accuse me of being too harsh and even cruel. I'm just starting to understand that maybe I was.

I always had low self-esteem as a kid. I couldn't do anything to please my dad. He would criticize everything I did. Once I made him a shoe rack at school for Christmas. His first comment was to tell me how I should have made it differently. I thought I was a bad person and felt a lot of shame. After all, if even my dad didn't like me, how could I expect others to? Fathers love their sons; if mine didn't, it must be because I was unlovable.

When my wife challenged my behavior with the children, it made me angry that I couldn't even be looked up to in my own home. Now it was supposed to be *my* turn to have people's respect and obedience. The more I tried to control my family, the worse things got. I talked to our preacher who said I was right in demanding obedience. He helped me see that the problem was my wife's lack of submission to my spiritual authority. Until she learned how to submit, I couldn't be free to lead. I tried to get her to go talk to him so he could explain that to her, but she refused.

I became more and more frustrated that my authority was being questioned in my very own home. I got angrier at my wife for not letting me be the man of the house. I have a niece who was twelve years old at the time, and I'd always had a close relationship with her. When I'd get mad at my wife, I'd go pick up my niece and take her out for ice cream. Since her father died when she was little, she enjoyed it when I did fatherly things with her. Her mother was always grateful too.

The trips to the ice cream store became more frequent. Then I started taking her miniature golfing and for rides in the car. My own kids were jealous of all the attention she was getting, but I explained it by saying "She at least appreciates me."

I must admit I started having funny feelings inside whenever I'd think about my niece. I also started fantasizing about snuggling up in bed with her in the nude. When we'd be together, I began touching her more and would keep my hand on her leg in the car. We'd always kissed good-bye, but now I began kissing her in a different way. My sister (her mother) did ask once how my own family felt about all the time I was spending with my niece. I assured my sister it was okay with my family. My sister, of course, had no way of knowing my feelings about her daughter had become sexual.

I still don't understand how it happened, but one night on the way home from miniature golfing, I drove to a secluded spot. I told my niece I wanted to teach her something about men and women that her daddy would have taught her if he were alive. Because my niece totally trusted and believed me, I had little trouble getting her to take off her clothes.

That was the first of many times we had intercourse in the back of my car. Several times she asked if I was sure this was all right to be doing. I told her it was what people did who loved each other, and since we loved each other, it was okay. I was able to overcome her verbal and physical resistance.

The next part of the story is a nightmare for me. One day at her school, the teacher talked about inappropriate touching. She asked the children if they'd ever been touched in ways that made them uncomfortable. At recess my niece talked to her teacher about the things I'd been doing to her. The teacher then called my sister.

My sister showed up at my work and told me to get in her car right away. She began crying and yelling and hitting me. She gave me an ultimatum—either I promised never to be alone with my niece again and get counseling or she would have the police arrest me. Getting counseling seemed less terrible than getting hauled down to the police station, so that was what I chose.

I'm just beginning to understand how I violated my niece's trust in me and how I took advantage of the power I had over her. But there's still a lot I don't understand.

A frequent response to the sexual abuse of children is confusion and bafflement. "How could an adult, who is supposed to naturally love and protect a child, ever do something like that?" Over the years, social scientists and psychotherapists have developed complicated theories with fancy names to explain why men sexually abuse children. The key explanation, I believe, is actually quite simple and straightforward. *Men sexually abuse because our patriarchal society implicitly condones the abuse of women and children and men believe they can get away with it.*

This chapter will briefly discuss the major theories of perpetration which have been proposed so that readers will be able to recognize them in the future and think critically about such explanations. As you read the different theories proposed to explain why men abuse children, remember that no matter what the circumstances of the abuse, it is always the abuser's fault. The abuser chose to abuse and is responsible for the assault.

Sexual abuse is to a large extent about the abuse of power and trust. It is to a much lesser degree about sexual issues. Still, the sexual component of abuse needs to be acknowledged. All sexual behavior, healthy and pathological, is complex and multifaceted. There are sexual and nonsexual motivations and needs in all sexual acts. In the healthy marital relationship, nonsexual components of the sex act may include the desire for closeness, for affirmation of specialness, or to confirm one's femininity or masculinity. In an unhealthy sexual relationship, nonsexual motivation may include the desire to humiliate, to control or overpower, to punish or retaliate.

While a significant motivation of a particular abuser may have been the need to dominate and control, the fact that these needs became sexualized must be considered. If the erotic component had been insignificant, the offender's needs to dominate and control might have been met in other, nonsexual ways. These might have included controlling the child's choice of clothing, friends, and activities; locking the child in a bedroom; or chaining her to a post.

## Erotic Factors Theories

*Pedophilia* is a term used to describe people who have a deviant sexual interest in children. The pedophile may have sexual contact with a child (meaning the person touches the child or has the child touch him to cause sexual arousal) or may masturbate to conscious fantasies involving children. Most pedophilic attraction begins in adolescence.

*Ephebophilia* is a sexual attraction to children in the budding stages of puberty. Some ephebophiles are attracted to adolescent boys, others to adolescent girls. Pedophiles and ephebophiles may be attracted to both adults and children but usually are more sexually aroused by children. Many are married. Many admit in treatment that they fantasize about children while having sexual relations with adults.

Why would an adult find a prepubescent child sexually arousing? Again, numerous theories have evolved to explain this phenomena. John Money (1986) has developed the concept of "lovemap" which is like a picture or template in an individual's mind/brain that depicts the idealized lover and what the person does with that lover in an erotic sexualized relationship. While there may be hormonal influences present at birth which affect the lovemap, it usually forms during the first eight years of life and most often results in sexual attraction to someone of the opposite sex of approximately the same age.

Money says that if children are forbidden to touch their bodies in erotically stimulating ways, are subjected to abusive punishment and discipline, or are exposed too abruptly to inappropriate sexualized behavior, the formation of their lovemap may be traumatized and damaged. This may result in deviant sexual arousal patterns and behaviors which manifest themselves after puberty and may include the sexual attraction to children.

This lovemap forms in complex ways not fully in control of an individual. But no matter what the idealized lover in a person's mind may be, it is *never* acceptable to use a vulnerable, defenseless child for gratification. Those with deviant lovemaps must and can learn to control their impulses and behavior so children and other vulnerable people are not hurt.

A related theory is that some people have early sexual experiences that model for them the option as adults to find children sexually arousing. Perhaps what is significant for abusers who were themselves abused as children is not that they were abused—but that they had a model of someone who found children sexually stimulating. This process may also operate in people who observed siblings or cousins being sexually exploited.

McGuire, Carlisle, and Young (1965) believe that the early experience of having seen a model who found children sexually stimulating becomes a fixation when incorporated into a masturbatory fantasy repeated over time. Because masturbation is pleasurably reinforcing, thoughts of children come to be associated with sexual arousal.

Many perpetrators admit that they have eroticized children by projecting sexual fantasies onto the mental image of children's bodies and masturbating to the images. Even after overt sexual involvement with children has begun, perpetrators report frequent fantasies about children combined with masturbation.

Fear of being caught abusing children increases production of adrenaline. This, coupled with the intensity of masturbatory fantasies, may result in heightened sexual stimulation. This intoxicatingly "high" feeling leads to an addictive pattern for some abusers. They become willing to risk the well-being of a child and their own reputation and family security for the sake of the momentary high of sexual involvement with a child. Sexual addictive tendencies must be fought and controlled just like the tendency to abuse substances must be controlled. "My addiction made me do it" is never a valid excuse for abusing a child.

A related theory is that sexual arousal to children may result from exposure to child pornography or other erotic media depictions of children. Exposure to sexually explicit depictions of children involved in sex acts with adults may increase the legitimacy and remove inhibitions about adult-child sexual behavior (Densen-Gerber, 1983; Russell, 1982). This hypothesis has not been tested extensively.

Another theory is that of arrested psychosocial development. According to this theory, child sex abusers are emotionally immature and find children sexually stimulating because they are at a similar emotional level (Hammer and Glueck, 1957; Groth and Birnbaum, 1978; Bell and Hall, 1976). Proponents of this theory say that child sexual abusers are ineffective in peer social relationships. The abusers may experience a better "fit," or more emotional congruence, between their emotional need and the child's characteristics.

Abusers are more likely than nonabusers to manifest low self-esteem, self-doubt, self-alienation, need for reinforcement, insecurity, and fear of heterosexual failure with an adult woman. In relationships with children, they may feel comparatively powerful and successful (Loss and Glancy, 1983). Even proponents of this theory point out that although a child may feel to the abuser like a better emotional "fit," this in no way excuses or justifies using a child for the gratification of an adult.

The family dynamics model of incestuous abuse supports the "blockage" model. For a variety of reasons, the marital relationship may have broken down. Sexual frustration and deprivation result when the physical, intimate relationship among spouses is unsatisfactory. Father may be too inhibited or "religious" to seek sexual satisfaction in an extramarital affair or through masturbation.Because all acceptable avenues for sexual expression with adults are "blocked," father may turn to his child to express his sexual needs. This is sometimes called the sexual deprivation/frustration theory.

But no matter how great the marital discord, no matter how "deprived" sexually a parent may be, sexually abusing a child can never be justified. Sexual deprivation and marital frustration are red herrings which do not adequately explain real reasons men abuse children. To focus on them will cause us to miss deeper reasons men abuse.

Howells (1981) theorizes that "attributional error" may be involved for those who find children sexually arousing. Many people have a strong, positive emotional response to children which is usually understood to be "parental," "affectionate," or "protective." Some people, Howells says, may erroneously interpret these feelings as sexual and respond accordingly. This theory seems to interpret the motivation of abusers through rosy glasses. Howells doesn't explain how these individuals can overcome moral constraints and use vulnerable people for their own pleasure.

## Nonerotic Factors Theories

To explain the motivation to abuse children sexually, non-erotic factors have also been explored by theorists and often highlighted by abusers.

Abusers frequently try to mitigate their responsibility for abuse by citing the many problems they face. In the abuser's mind, marital discord, loss of a job, or a sick wife may fully explain sexual involvement with a child. One incestuous father "apologized" to his ten-year-old daughter, saying,

> I'm sorry to be doing this to you. I know it's not your fault but it isn't mine either. With your mom pregnant again and me out of work, I can't see that I have any other choice. Look at it this way, it's your part in saving the family. At least I'm not out picking up someone at a bar or running around with some other young thing. When I get my job back and my pride restored, this will stop.

It is not surprising that many men blame their wives for their own sexually abusive behavior. Ours is a culture, and psychology is a profession, with long traditions of blaming women, particularly mothers, for everything from impotence to schizophrenia to homosexuality.

Many abusers have difficulty identifying feelings. If you ask what they are feeling, they are more likely to tell you what they are thinking. They appear genuinely ignorant of their feelings at any given moment. Likewise, abusers can't tolerate such feelings as anger, frustration, or depression without resorting to sexual acts to release the tension created by the feelings.

There are indications that in general in our culture, men more than women may channel expressions of feelings through their sexual organs. And the perpetrator, even more than many men, lacks ability to understand what he is feeling. He rarely has close friends with whom he can share deep emotional pain but instead tends to be emotionally isolated. Instead of facing his fears and anxieties, the perpetrator sexualizes these feelings and tries to make himself feel better by becoming sexual with a child.

Many professionals have noted that perpetrators turn to incest in an unsuccessful attempt to meet their emotional as well as sexual needs (see Maltz and Holman, 1987). But it is questionable whether any abuser can genuinely convince himself that it is somehow acceptable to abuse his daughter because he is feeling depressed. And of course, even if he can fool himself, there is no ethical justification for abusing a child.

The "identification with the aggressor" theory maintains that abusers, in an attempt to overcome the effects of their own childhood abuse, defuse their own trauma by reversing roles in the victimization. In a bizarre sense, the molester may feel he can overcome the humiliation of "childhood-induced psychological traumas" which he may have experienced as a child.

Finkelhor says "they combat their own powerlessness by becoming the powerful victimizer" (1986, p. 95). However, my psychiatrist friend Scott Walker believes that persons victimized as children have many options for behavior in adulthood. These may cluster around three major categories—become a sheep (helpless prey to further victimization), a shepherd (caretaker of others), or a wolf (victimizer of others).

Victims of abuse have options for living out their adult lives. Abusing others is only one inexcusable option. Many survivors I know are *less* likely than nonabused peers to abuse a child. As a friend says, "I know how devastating it has been for me to have been abused; there is no way I would ever do that to another child!"

A legitimate and useful theoretical framework for understanding perpetrators is Albert Bandura's (1977) social-learning theory. Bandura highlights the impact of modeling on learning. He observes that direct reinforcement of behavior is not the only way by which human beings learn. Learning can occur through observation and example.

In a famous experiment, Bandura had preschool children observe an adult model playing with "Bobo," an inflated plastic figure. The adult model kicked, hit, and beat with a hammer the plastic Bobo. Later when the children were allowed to play with Bobo, they too kicked, hit, and beat the plastic figure. The children imitated the model's aggressive and violent behavior toward Bobo even when the model was only seen on film or in a cartoon.

Further experiments have found that children are even more likely to imitate the model's behavior if the model is perceived by the children to have high status. Examples of high status models include parents, movie stars, rock stars, athletes, or famous cartoon characters.

In their homes, the media, and society in general, boys may have modeled for them behavior which devalues women and children, which is violent toward females and objectifies them. Through such modeling, boys "learn" this is the way males act toward females. Through observation and imitation of other abusive males, boys learn to be perpetrators.

## Conservative Religiosity and Abuse

A disturbing fact continues to surface in sex abuse research. The first best predictor of abuse is alcohol or drug addiction in the father. But the second best predictor is conservative religiosity, accompanied by parental belief in traditional female-male roles. This means that if you want to know which children are most likely to be sexually abused by their father, the second most significant clue is *whether or not the parents belong to a conservative religious group with traditional role beliefs and rigid sexual attitudes* (Brown and Bohn, 1989; Finkelhor, 1986; Fortune, 1983; Goldstein, Kant, and Hartman, 1973; Van Leeuwen, 1990).

How is this possible? Why aren't children in a religious home safer from abuse than children in a nonreligious home? What is it about conservative religious homes which actually puts children at greater risk of being sexually abused by their father?

Persons whose beliefs are conservative may have many strong, healthy characteristics which deserve respect and affirmation. But because of ways they may contribute to abuse, those qualities of conservatism which are potentially negative will be focused on here.

People with rigid personality structures may be attracted to churches with firm belief systems. When a person sees everything in terms of absolute right and absolute wrong, there is less flexibility in thinking and behavior. If a man has been taught he must be the unquestionable head of the family and his wife and children should live in submission to him, he may feel more threatened when this identity and role is challenged.

Having identified strongly with a prescribed role in the family, the man may in fact be less aware of who he truly is as a feeling person apart from that role. The more persons lack a clear sense of personal individuality beyond a prescribed role, the less able they are to see children as separate and unique persons. Such persons have difficulty respecting and valuing children for their own intrinsic worth and not just as extensions of parental needs.

When a man believes it is his God-given right and responsibility to control his wife and children, he may logically assume justification for using any means necessary to maintain that control. Furthermore, he may come to believe he owns them. And if he owns them, then, of course, he should be able to do whatever he wants to them.

As is true of men raised in any environment which tends to repress sexuality, men in conservative religious homes are often obsessed with sexual thoughts and feelings but rarely share these with others. Because they may consider sexual thoughts dirty and sinful, they become ashamed and afraid of them. The more they try to repress these powerful urges and thoughts, the more powerful they become. Sexual feelings and thoughts may seem to take on a life of their own, which feels out of the control of the legalistic Christian man.

And so the circle becomes vicious. The more the man thinks about sexual matters, the more shame he feels. The more shame he feels the harder he tries to repress and deny these feelings. The more he tries to repress and deny them, the more energy they have. And then the more shame he feels, and the harder he tries to deny the urges, the more powerful they become, and on and on.

Beliefs in legalistic religious homes tend to be exclusivistic. Such families believe their way of believing and living is the Right Way; those who hold different beliefs are going the Wrong Way. Affirmation of the right way a family has chosen can be a positive, empowering quality. But obsessive commitment to the right way may lead to a judgmental mentality.

Most significantly, rigidly exclusivistic beliefs create an environment of "us and them" and build a moat of separatism and isolation around the family behind which abuse can flourish undetected by others. In families where abuse is committed, the boundaries which isolate them from the outside world are very rigid. The family's shame and the perpetrator's need for secrecy to protect the ugly secrets and continue the abuse isolate both the family and the victim from the outside world.

In a healthy family, the boundaries between members are strong but permeable enough that communication and intimate sharing may occur. Each family member has a sense of her or his own identity, rights, and needs as a unique individual. Members of a healthy family are able to get close to each other in love and intimacy but are likewise able to pull back as a separate individual, each with a unique identity, when appropriate.

In a family where abuse occurs, the boundaries between family members tend to be loose, with individual needs getting blurred into one blended neediness. The perpetrator isolates the victim from other people outside the family, then tells her through his behavior that she has no individual worth or rights except to meet his needs. He destroys her personal emotional and physical boundaries and convinces her he can touch and use her whenever he wants because she has no rights of her own.

## Male Socialization

Physical abuse of children is committed approximately equally by men and women. However, after adjusting for which parent the child more often lives with and which has most responsibility for childcare, the level of physical abuse by fathers is higher than that by mothers (Creighton, 1987). Victims are about equally male and female.

Physical abuse is considered primarily a problem of poor parenting skills. When caretakers are unable to respond in nonviolent, creative ways to children's misbehavior or childishness, or when they don't know appropriate ways of dealing with stress and frustration, they may resort to physical abuse.

Sexual abuse is committed primarily by heterosexual men against girls. Men have far less contact with children than women. Men are rarely primary caregivers and even more rarely sole caregivers of children. Yet about 90 percent of perpetrators of sexual abuse are male. Increasingly, sexual abuse of children is regarded as a problem of male socialization.

Humans are born female or male. They must learn to be feminine or masculine. Theorists such as Carol Gilligan (1982), Nancy Chodorow (1974), and Robert Stoller (1964) have helped document this process.

All theories about male and female socialization are gradually being updated by changes in society and ongoing research. No one really can be sure how gender issues will be understood a generation from now, when the current ferment in gender roles may have yielded new insights and even socialization practices.

But as researchers have tried to make sense of past gender understandings and ways men and women have been socialized, many theories have addressed the tendency in North American society for the primary childcare giver to be female. Consequently, most girls learn about being feminine by being like and affiliating with their primary caregivers—females. Thus their very conception of self is rooted in a sense of connectedness and relatedness to others.

In contrast, some theorists believe male identity has developed in boys as they are different than and separate from their mothers, their primary caretakers. The important male in the boy's life, usually his father, traditionally spent little time each day relating personally and directly to his son. Consequently, male identity has been rooted in the experience of not being like his primary caregiver, being separate from her, and needing to pull away and be different from her.

This is changing in some circles, but a generation ago (and still often today), boys seen as emotionally too close to their mothers were labeled "sissy" or "mother's boy." When asked what it meant to be female, little girls traditionally tended to list positive behaviors such as "be gentle" and "take good care of little children." Boys, however, listed such negatives as "don't be weak," "don't cry," "don't be a sissy."

Thus male identity has tended to be negative. The cultural assumptions and practices which have traditionally made childcare a female responsibility have damaged males and ultimately all of us. Since boys develop a sense of maleness through separation, though being different from their mothers and not doing the things mothers do, some males are threatened by intimacy. Males often have more difficulty with close relationships than do females. Their very identity as males is sometimes threatened by emotional intimacy.

On the other hand, many men are more adept than many females at relating to others on an impersonal, objective basis. They may thus have less difficulty accepting others as separate and individual. Related to this process is the North American male's tendency to be less emotional and personal about sexual behavior. Women find it difficult to separate the sex act from the total relationships. But many men are socialized to separate sexually intimate behavior from the overall context of relationship. This in turn makes it more likely that men will sexualize relationships which should not be sexualized.

When boys learn that being male means being different from mother, they may receive subtle encouragement to reject affectionate, nurturing behaviors considered maternal. They may feel pushed to become dominant, strong, aggressive. They may feel urged to control other people and their own emotions. From birth, boys are encouraged to be strong, brave, and not cry. Our society traditionally has had inhumane expectations of males which hurt all of us.

A client stated that his father had never complimented him nor expressed pride in him. "Oh, I take that back," he said. "One day in school a classmate hit me in the stomach; I jumped him, threw him to the ground, and smashed my fist in his face."

His father was called to the principal's office to meet his son and the other boy. The other boy's eyes were black and blue and his nose swollen and bleeding. After hearing the details of the altercation, "my father for the first and last time in my life said, 'I'm proud of you, son!' "

Another man tells of the humiliation he felt as a young boy when he was afraid of being alone in his dark room at night. After several nights of running to his parent's room for comfort, his father one day made him wear his sister's dress, hair bow, shoes, and socks, and forced him to walk around their block three times. His father's angry greeting when the boy returned from the humiliating exercise was "I hope that teaches you not to act like a crybaby girl!" What it *did* teach him was that it isn't safe or appropriate for boys to express fear, weakness, or vulnerability.

Because boys, like girls, experience a broad range of feelings, males have often learned to deny and suppress many emotions. When told only little girls or crybabies (not *real* men) act sad or scared or weak, boys learn to mask and hide feelings even from themselves. Thus can begin a pattern of denial and repression leading to lack of self-awareness and self-understanding. This makes it difficult for men to recognize and acknowledge their intimate needs and unfulfilled yearnings and contributes to their vulnerability to inappropriate sexual relationships.

Years of inhibiting feelings out of fear of not measuring up to acceptable standards of masculinity can cause adult men to be less aware of their emotions and less willing to disclose them. Although this is changing as society re-evaluates gender roles, the male role as traditionally defined by our culture required men to be tough, unsentimental, and emotionally unexpressive. If men's feelings didn't match these standards, they were nonetheless expected to act tough.

Men who feel obliged to deny tender feelings may be less inclined to accept responsibility for their relationships with weaker and more vulnerable persons. A man who hasn't learned to face and feel his own sense of vulnerability and woundedness, may find it impossible to face and feel that in others. Years of inhibition of feelings take their toll in men. Denial of feelings affects men's ability to have insight and empathy toward themselves and others. It causes a tendency for male sexual behavior to be more influenced by artificial gender role expectations than by authentic personal feelings.

We have come to understand that the human organism longs for and needs physical touch to thrive. Yet males in our culture have been allowed few opportunities for touching. A fear of being considered homosexual or effeminate confines touching between many men (unless drunk) to rough playing, a hand jive or handshake, an occasional pat on the back, an infrequent arm around the shoulder, or a rambunctious whack on the rear during sporting events.

Men have lacked opportunities to express nurturing, tender feelings except in sex. They have been taught that the manly way to express care and to seek warmth is through sexual activity. If they want to express affection and tenderness, men may, because of limited touching skills, resort to overt sexual activity when a hug or gentle hand squeeze might be more appropriate and better fulfill their true needs.

Because men have usually been given fewer opportunities than women to practice affectionate behaviors outside of sexual encounters, men tend to look to sex, even with such inappropriate sexual partners as children, to meet these needs. Likewise men are more inclined than women to define affectionate exchanges as sexual and to become sexually aroused by them.

Another socialization factor related to sexual abuse by men against little girls is our traditional cultural stress on male dominance in relationships. We have encouraged men to take charge, to be dominant and powerful in relationships at work, in church, and in the home. The masculine role has called for men to dominate and control women and children.

Men have been particularly socialized to be dominant in sexual relationships. Women have been socialized to see older, larger, stronger people as appropriate sexual partners; men have been socialized to see younger, weaker, smaller people as appropriate. Children are a gross extension of these male sexual partner standards. These standards make children vulnerable to sexual abuse by adult men.

Diana Russell (1986) has observed that males have often been socialized with a predatory approach to obtaining sexual gratification, which predisposes them to sexual violence and sexual abuse. Jane Caputi (1987) and Joan Smith (1989) have likewise noted the connection in our culture between male sexuality and violence. It is indeed becoming clear to many that in our society men's violence is often normalized, naturalized, and eroticized.

The connection between sex and violence is made early in little boys. A friend who works at a daycare center tells of the rhyme a four-year-old-boy, one hand forming a gun held near his chest and the other hand forming a gun held by his penis, told in her presence one day.

This is a rifle, this is a gun;
This is for fighting, this is for fun.

Not surprisingly, another friend tells me this chant originated with the military and is used in boot camps. Men have passed on to me other military ditties which likewise reflect a disturbing connection between war, sex and, violence toward women and children.

Many men have been taught that true manhood is proved through successful performance in heterosexual sex acts. Men's identity and egos are closely tied to their ability to attract sex partners and to perform the sex act. But men are caught in a cultural double bind because good women aren't supposed to enjoy sex!

Many men have told me that when their pride gets hurt and their egos battered, they turn to sex as confirmation that they are "still a man." It matters little to the abusive man that the only available sexual partner is an inappropriate choice, such as a child. The important thing for such a man is to convince himself that despite assault to his male ego he remains a man.

The term commonly used for erectile dysfunction in men is "impotence." This means "without power." A man who cannot have or maintain an erection or cannot ejaculate is seen as powerless. Because maleness, power, and aggressive sexual behavior are so strongly associated in our culture, a sexually impotent man may find his very sense of manhood greatly damaged.

Some men in our culture find submissive behavior erotically stimulating. For a man experiencing erectile problems, a submissive young, small, weak child may be particularly sexually arousing to him. Suppose he experiences his wife as a powerful person, considers her a "castrating witch," and erroneously blames her for his erectile problems. Then he may see relatively powerless children to whom he has access as potential submissive sex partners. Perhaps with them he can regain his erectile ability and restore his sense of power and masculinity.

We will not stop sexual abuse of children until we challenge and change the profound and damaging violence of traditional cultural patterns of male socialization. Chapters 10 and 11 discuss steps congregations can take to encourage and model a healthier, more Christlike way of being a man. The following chapter examines religious beliefs which, in interaction with other factors, appear related to abuse.

# Chapter 5
# Religious Beliefs and Abuse

Most of us can think of devout, religious people who are happy, kind, and emotionally healthy. Most of us also can name religious, devout people who are among the most opinionated, rigid, and hateful people we know.

While spiritual resources and religious beliefs can enable humans to live godly, healthy lives, it isn't enough just to believe. It makes a difference *what* people believe. In the early years of this century, Christian psychologist William James observed that, to determine if religious beliefs were help or hindrance to mentally healthy living, it was important to distinguish between various kinds of religious beliefs (James, 1932).

In subsequent years, other social psychologists spoke of two different ways of being religious. In one way, religion was used to justify self-centered ends, while in another, religious commitments were thoughtfully made and incorporated into the larger context and personal goals of life. Gordon Allport made the distinction between intrinsic and extrinsic religion. *Extrinsically* motivated people, Allport says, *use* their religion. *Intrinsically* motivated people *live* their religion (Allport, 1950).

Thomas Adorno (1950) observed that many religious people supported Hitler. He wanted to understand what kind of religious person was attracted to Nazism. Adorno, like Allport, identified different ways of being religious. The first way Adorno called *neutralized* religion. In people whose religion was neutralized, Adorno saw lack of understanding of the deeper spiritual claims of religion. This was accompanied by dogmatic, rigid clinging to doctrine. People with neutralized religion tend to "make use of religious ideas in order to gain some immediate practical advantage or to aid in the manipulation of other people" (Adorno, Frenkel-Brunswik, Levinson, and Sanford, 1950, p. 733). The second way of being religious, according to Adorno, involves personally experienced beliefs which are internalized in the person's life.

Jesus understood different ways of being religious. He criticized highly religious people who followed the letter of the law but ignored deeper spiritual truths. He understood that some religious beliefs and practices are used to manipulate appearances and to dehumanize people.

It is disturbing to know that many abusers of children are highly religious. Some of us working in the field of sexual abuse have observed common religious beliefs which seem to be related to the incidence of abuse. This is not to say that any one of these beliefs *causes* sexual abuse. However, certain beliefs seem to interact with other factors to provide an environment where abuse can occur. In such an environment would-be abusers find it possible to justify their behavior through distortion or extension of religious teachings, and victims find it difficult to stop the abuse. This chapter examines six beliefs often present in abusive environments.

**1. *God intends for men to dominate and women and children to submit.*** A belief which appears related to abuse is the teaching that domination of men over women and children is part of God's original plan for families and other male-female relationships. Subordination to men is understood as a creation ordinance laid out in Genesis 2. In the Genesis 2 creation account,

Adam is formed first, from dust. Then the animals are created and Adam names them as a symbol of his authority and dominion over them. Woman is created from man, to be his helper and, like the animals, is named by man.

Many see this version of creation as establishing a divinely ordained dominance-submission model of human relations in which men are to be in authority over women and children. The resultant theology of ownership has pervaded the biblical tradition, in which women and children are often regarded as property of men. The Pentateuch (Exod. 20:17 and Deut. 5:21, for example) includes a man's wife among his possessions, along with slaves, animals, house, and land. In biblical times a man owned his daughter and could sell her just as any other property.

I have observed that many abusive families are genuinely surprised to have the Genesis 1 creation story pointed out to them. Here male and female are created simultaneously and given equal responsibility for interacting with the rest of creation. Both are depicted as having been created in the image of God. Both are seen as the pinnacle of God's creation.

But many contemporary books written by Christian authors on family relations and marriage are based on the Genesis 2 account. Among arguments derived from this text are these:

- Woman was created after the man and is therefore secondary to him.
- Woman was taken from the man and is therefore secondary to him.
- Woman was named by the man and is therefore subordinate to him.
- Woman was created to be a helper for man and as such is subordinate to him.

This application of the Genesis 2 account is questionable. There does not appear to be legitimate justification for dependency and subservience of women based on this text. The tone of this chapter seems to be on comparability between woman and man. Even though the animals were interesting and varied, Adam needed someone *like himself* to be happy and fulfilled. To say that because Eve was created to be Adam's helper she is second-ary and subservient to him seems to misinterpret the intent of the passage.

As evangelical scholar Van Leeuwen (1990) notes, the He-brew word for "helper" used in Genesis 2 is frequently employed in the Old Testament to speak of God. Two examples of this usage are found in Psalms 70:5 and Psalms 121:2. Instead of interpreting the Genesis 2 account as saying woman is sec-ondary to man, Phyllis Trible (1978) suggests it is more accurate to regard woman as the helper corresponding to the man, as one who walks and works beside him because she is like him in ev-ery essential way as part of the image of God.

The name for the social organization and set of beliefs which grant and sustain male power and control over women and chil-dren is *patriarchy*. Relationships in a patriarchy are defined in terms of domination of men and submission of women and chil-dren.

The inherent logic of patriarchy says that if men have the right to power and control over women and children, they also have the right to enforce that control. It is this *control-over* component of patriarchy which makes it vulnerable to violence and abuse, not just against women and children but also against the earth and its resources. Domination and glorification of violence are characteristic of patriarchal societies. Men who don't conform to this are considered effeminate (Eisler, 1987).

In patriarchy, women and children are defined in relation to men who control the resources and power. Women and children are the other, the object. Men are the norm, the subject. In a dominance-and-submission social order, there is no true mutual care. Subordinates are to care for the needs of the dominants.

Patriarchy stands in contrast to the Genesis picture of the Creator's intent for male-female relations. It is instead the model Genesis 3 warns will result from sin entering the world and dis-torting human relationships. Through sin, God's plan for mutual submission and dominion over the earth becomes male domina-tion and control and female relinquishment of responsibility to help exercise dominion.

What is presented in Genesis as *descriptive* and *predictive* of the results of sin entering the world and perverting human relationships has been interpreted by some as *prescriptive* of what ought to be. Even though other results of the Fall (weeds and labor pains, for example) have been minimized or fought against, some Christians maintain that God's intentions as prescribed in Genesis are for men to dominate in social relationships.

In recent years some religious leaders and politicians alike have spoken nostalgically of the need to return to a traditional family model. This is equated with the biblical, Christian model. Books, radio shows, seminars, and televangelists make it clear that the traditional, biblical model they envision consists of a father who heads the family and works outside the home, and a nonpaid mother who submits to her husband and makes home and children top priority until the children leave home. At that point the wife may consider outside employment if she is still able to make home her top priority and if her husband approves the arrangement.

Interestingly, this model of being a family is not particularly a biblical model but reflects more the urbanization and industrialization trends which began in the nineteenth century (Laslett, 1972). Before this, men, women, and children worked around the home together, sharing nurturing tasks and economic undertakings.

Teachings in some Christian churches regarding marriage and family life are based on certain selected Scriptures and reflect a patriarchal, dominance-submission model of human relationships. Some Christian teachers warn that evil forces (usually identified as either communist or secular humanist) are at work to destroy America and that the strategy is to demolish the traditional family (LaHaye, 1980 and Falwell, 1981).

Christian families are urged to return to the so-called biblical model, to follow the appropriate "chain of command" hierarchy, the divine order of authority (Gothard, 1975). Social order, according to this view, demands the authority of men over women and children. The appropriate relationship between genders is one of rule and obedience, of dominance and submission.

Though there are many accounts in the Bible of families which operated according to this dominance-and-submission pattern, we must beware of equating this style with God's intentions. Just because a model appears in the Bible doesn't mean it is the model God intended or desires for human families. As Gretchen Gaebelein Hull (1987) notes, the Bible is the "true record of a false idea." The Bible is a startlingly accurate picture of fallen humanity.

In Jesus we see modeled a way of treating women and children which returns to God's original intentions for human relationships. Jesus models for us interpersonal relationships which reflect the new creation. This Jesus model should be lifted up as the desirable Christian pattern for human interactions. Models of interpersonal relationships rooted in dominance-submission violate Jesus' teachings. Matthew 20:20-28 suggests that hierarchical authority structures are typical of the way pagans organize social relationships—but should not characterize Jesus' followers. Ephesians 5:21—6:9 reflects a revolutionary shift from patriarchy to mutuality and foreshadows the radical equality of all in Christ which is summarized in Galatians 3:28.

As long as a patriarchy is supported and male dominance is considered the appropriate model for human relationships, sexual abuse of children will continue. It is impossible both to stop sexual abuse and to support a patriarchal family model. This position distresses those who are convinced patriarchy is the biblical model for families but care deeply about sexual abuse.

Christian scholars have done some creative thinking which can help us out of our quagmire. Mennonite theologian Willard Swartley offers guidelines for using the Bible to solve current ethical questions. He identifies as a strength the Bible's "missionary principle," which is the constant modification of its message to people in different cultural settings and times (Swartley, 1983).

The biblical story of salvation may be seen as

> an unfolding drama in which God's salvation is made available to more and more groups previously considered marginal. Salvation and equality of access to its privileges and responsibilities, is not just for Jews, but for non-Jews; not just for free persons, but for slaves; not just for men, but for women—and so on, in keeping

with the principle Paul enunciated in his original letter to the Galatians (3:28) (Van Leeuwen, 1990, p. 234).

Swartley suggests the following questions be used when doing biblical interpretation.

1. How are the two Testaments related?
2. How is the authority of Jesus related to all of Scripture?
3. What is the relationship between divine revelation and the culture in which the revelation is given and perceived?
4. Does Scripture mandate, regulate, or challenge some practices associated with slavery, war, and the subordination of women?
5. Does the Bible say only one thing on a given subject, or does it sometimes show differing, even contradictory points of view?
6. What does it mean to take the Bible literally? Is that vice or a virtue? Does "literal" signify the intended meaning of the author or a meaning that seems natural to us?
7. To what extent do the interpreter's predetermined positions, even ideologies, affect the interpretive task? (Swartley, 1983, p. 21).

Swartley's chapter "The Bible and Women" provides scriptural alternatives to patriarchy. Several other excellent books are available which are sensitive to both the Bible and current social science understandings of gender-related issues. In *Beyond Sex Roles: What the Bible Says About a Woman's Place in Church and Family*, Wheaton professor Gilbert Bilezikian methodically goes through Scripture and examines what the Bible says and doesn't say about the role of women. In *Gender and Grace: Love, Work and Parenting in a Changing World*, Mary Stewart Van Leewen suggests that the Bible points beyond patriarchy to a vision of mutuality between brothers and sisters in Christ.

**2. *Because of her role in the Fall, woman is morally inferior to man.*** Another religious belief that has surfaced in my clinical and research experience with the abused is that because of Eve's role in the Fall, woman is more vulnerable to spiritual deception than man and is morally defective. Because of this, woman should submit to man, who is more capable of making valid moral decisions.

Many Christian writers and teachers support this belief. In her book, *Me? Obey Him?* Handford (1972, p. 17) says, "Women are more often led into spiritual error than men. That is the reason God commanded her not to usurp authority over man, so she can be protected by him, from false doctrine." A woman who believes this finds it hard to trust herself and her judgments.

In both men and women, a connection has been found between the association of femininity with sinfulness and defectiveness and masculinity with divinity. Many people do believe that guillible Eve fell for the serpent's smooth talk. She tricked poor Adam into eating of the forbidden fruit and is thus solely responsible for the entry of sin into the world. Many also believe that ever since woman has been more susceptible to deception.

Christian women are given seemingly contradictory messages. On the one hand is the fundamental Christian teaching of the dignity and worth of each human and the message that Christianity has elevated women to unprecedented heights of honor. On the other hand, women are taught that because of Eve's sin they themselves are morally, defective and are to live in subordination to men.

Such teachings tend to reinforce the notion about woman's unchangeable inferiority, not merely physical but also intellectual and moral (Daly, 1975). A female who believes she is morally defective and thus unable to trust her sense that something is wrong in a given situation will find it hard to confront an abusive man, particularly if he tells her, "It's all in your head," or "You're just imagining things." When females can't trust themselves, they easily give up their power and ability to resist things done to them, particularly by a male.

Women in such families are expected to submit to the man's leadership and to support his behavior and decisions, whether or not she agrees with him. As head of the family, his authority and behavior are not to be questioned (LaHaye, 1980 and Handford, 1972). On the other hand, passivity, unassertiveness, and accommodating behaviors are encouraged in women.

Miller (1976) studied the psychological effects of dominance-submission relationships. In an attempt to survive, people in the subordinate position develop characteristics pleasing to people in dominance. These traits include submissiveness, passivity, docility, dependency, lack of initiative, and the inability to act, to decide, and to think for themselves.

These very qualities, which are encouraged in some conservative churches as appropriate for godly Christian woman, will not empower women to stop abusive man from battering them or violating children. Instead, these qualities make it difficult for women to protect either themselves or their children.

A colleague and I studied clergy beliefs about the personal qualities and behaviors which describe a spiritually healthy Christian woman (Long and Heggen, 1988). We found that indeed pastors from conservative churches described a spiritually healthy woman as "submissive in the home," "gentle and soft-spoken," "lets spouse make decisions," "dependent," "passive," "finds identity through spouse," and "withholds criticism." These qualities were not used by conservative pastors to describe a spiritually healthy male or adult of unspecified gender.

Because conservative churches teach that such qualities are important for a Christian woman, she may feel pressured to adopt attitudes and behaviors which detract from her ability to protect herself and her children from an abusive husband.

I have also studied the relationship between Christian women's beliefs about appropriate roles for men and women and women's level of self-esteem (Heggen, 1989). Women who believed in a traditional model of female subordination to men tended to have lower self-esteem scores than did women who believed in equality and partnership for men and women.

So what? Social scientists have repeatedly found a strong relationship between a person's self-esteem and their mental health (Bandura, 1977; Coopersmith, 1967; Pancheri and Benaissa, 1978; and Witmer, Rich, Barcikowski, and Mague, 1983). Self-esteem is critical for emotional well-being. People with low self-esteem cannot confront offensive behavior in others. Mothers with low self-esteem cannot effectively guard against abusive fathers.

In the male headship model, the wife tends to have little economic power. Women who don't trust their own judgments and are economically dependent on their husbands are reluctant to leave home no matter how violent and abusive their husbands. When she and her children must depend on the man's favor to survive economically, it becomes difficult for a woman to confront his inappropriate behavior. Though she knows he is abusive, he is her economic lifeline and she may see no options. Overlooking the abuse may seem preferable to a life on the streets with her children.

No wonder daughters in incestuous families often see their mothers as weak and powerless. As one survivor told me, "Mom didn't even have the authority to decide when she was going into town to do grocery shopping. I knew telling her about my abuse would just add to her frustrations. She didn't have enough power anyway to stop it."

Another woman said, "Mom was so emotionally beat down by Dad that she was the last person I would have seen as able to stop the abuse."

The mother of an abused daughter explained, "All those years when my daughter was little and being abused, I was so depressed and emotionally weak that I couldn't think about anything but my own pain. Now I realize that may have been part of his strategy. He knew that as long as I was depressed and dependent on him I wouldn't ever leave. That gave him lots of years of access to my daughter with no one strong enough to decisively question or stop his behavior."

**3. *Children are inherently evil and must have their wills broken*.** Many Christian parenting books and seminars reflect a strong belief in the inherent evil of children and the need to break their wills through physical punishment. This need to break the wills of children is a third belief often associated with abusive environments.

Parents are taught that unless their children obey and submit to the authority of their parents, they will never submit to God. Thus parents come to regard their children's eternal salvation as dependent on submitting to parental control. It should be no surprise that North American Protestants have always been among vocal defenders of physical punishment for children (Greven, 1990).

Even though corporal punishment cannot be justified by anything Jesus or the apostle Paul are recorded as having said, physical punishment and the infliction of pain on children are advocated as necessary tools of Christian discipline. Christian tradition has reinforced the belief that violence is an acceptable way to teach and enforce obedience.

Protestant bookstores are filled with books advocating physical punishment as God's will and a requirement for Christian parenting. Such books warn of the relationship between physical punishment and the development of morality, spirituality, character, and ultimately, the eternal salvation of children (Greven, 1990).

Popular Christian writers on parenting and family life matters such as James Dobson, Roy Lessin, and Larry Christenson have helpful things to say. They are also among those who encourage parents to inflict pain on their children when they disobey. For example, Christenson says, "God has ordained issues of the greatest importance to hinge upon the discipline of the rod—even involving the child's eternal salvation" (Christenson, p. 112, 1970).

Lessin says, "Spanking is God's idea. He is the one who has commanded parents to spank their children as an expression of love. Spanking is not optional" (Lessin, 1979, p. 30).

Dobson says that "pain is a marvelous purifier" and recommends that parents spank children to control their willfulness (Dobson, p. 13, 1970). In his updated *New Dare to Discipline,* Dobson still endorses spanking. In response to a question from a parent who wonders why spanking hasn't helped, Dobson responds, "The spanking may be too gentle. If it doesn't hurt it isn't worth avoiding next time" (Dobson, p. 72, 1992).

Children in Christian homes learn that to be good they must be obedient and submissive to the authority and will of their parents. The rewards are the biblical promise of a long life, the avoidance of pain and humiliation, and the affirmation and love of their parents. Children assume, sometimes incorrectly, that whatever their parents ask them to do is appropriate. Because of the strong emphasis on obedience and submission to parental will, especially father's, children from these homes may be more likely to submit to inappropriate and abusive sexual behavior from a parent.

Let me be clear. As mother of three young children, I *know* the importance of providing clear guidance and loving authority for my children. As a parent I am grateful that my children most often respect and obey me. For a family to function smoothly and happily, children must learn to respect our authority as their parents. But to make unqualified obedience to parents the central focus of child rearing is potentially damaging and inappropriate.

**4. *Marriages must be preserved at all cost*.** Christians have historically placed a high premium on the marital covenant, which is meant to provide a safe, stable, and loving environment for adults and children. When the covenant has been broken and the home instead becomes a place of violation and human destruction, the church has too often opted to preserve the pretense of covenant over the safety of violated people. This emphasis on marriage preservation at all costs is a fourth belief associated with abusive environments.

Churches have tended to value the permanence of marriage over the dignity and sanctity of personhood. Too often women and abused children have been told to return to an abusive home because "it's God's will," "you promised to stay with him till death do you part," or "God wants families to stay together." Of course God wants marriages to last and families to stay together.

But that's only part of the story. God wants homes to be places of emotional and physical safety. When they are instead the very places vulnerable people experience violation and abuse, and when the marriage covenant is broken by violence, the church must honestly and wisely struggle to find God's permissive will amidst human brokenness. Human beings must not be sacrificed on the altar of devotion to marital permanence. Maintaining a facade of marital well being must not take precedence over protecting vulnerable people. Before women and children are told to return to violent men, the church must do everything in its power to make sure the violator is confronted, his behavior changed and monitored, and the home made safe for all people.

**5. *Suffering is a Christian virtue.*** Ask people in any part of the world what the symbol of Christianity is and most will name the cross. The crucifixion has become the central image of Christianity. Christ's death on the cross has generally been regarded by Christians as vital to humankind's redemption from the effects of sin. Thus the cross may be seen appropriately as a symbol of the redemptive nature of Christ's suffering. Some, however, have made the cross a symbol of the virtue of *all* suffering. This has resulted in a glorification of suffering among some Christians and has created a fifth belief associated with abusive environments—that suffering is a Christian virtue. Martyrdom, an extreme form of suffering which results in death, has had a special place of honor in the Christian tradition since the time of Jesus.

In general, women within the Christian tradition have been chosen for the role of "suffering servant" and are considered capable of suffering more patiently, more nobly, than men. Women tend to see themselves as able to endure more emotional and physical pain than men. How often have we heard women bragging about their capacity to put up with more pain than their male counterparts? How often have we heard women say, "Thank goodness men don't have babies; they'd never be able to endure the pain"? How often have we heard women smugly joke about what big babies men are when sick?

In an atmosphere which glorifies suffering, females tend to see abuse as their cross to bear, as their way of identifying with the sufferings of Christ. This may result in a pattern of endurance which minimizes the offensiveness of abuse and fosters the acceptance of victimization.

Marie Fortune (1983) makes the important distinction between voluntary and involuntary suffering. Voluntary suffering is pain and affliction *chosen* to accomplish a greater good. Mahatma Gandhi, for example, chose to put himself in situations which he knew would cause him suffering. He chose suffering in the hope of changing situations and structures of oppression which caused suffering for many people. He didn't choose to suffer because there is something virtuous about suffering for suffering's sake. He chose to suffer because it might help bring justice, freedom, and dignity for his people.

Rosa Parks surely knew that by not going to the back of that Montgomery city bus in the mid-fifties she would bring suffering on herself. She didn't choose this action because she wanted to suffer. She chose it because she was willing to suffer as a way of bringing attention and change to dehumanizing, degrading practices and laws.

We must make a clear distinction between voluntarily suffering for a greater good and involuntary suffering which results from another person's sin against us and yields no greater good. Granted, in both kinds of suffering the victim may feel God's presence amidst pain. In both God may "sanctify . . . thy deepest distress," in the words of the popular hymn "How Firm a Foundation." We may come out of both kinds of suffering with an increased sensitivity to our own weakness and vulnerability and an increased reliance on God.

But we must not idealize the results of suffering. Many victims of involuntary suffering come out of the experience with crushed spirits and profound emotional and spiritual pain. Some lose their ability to believe in a just and powerful God who allows such devastating things to happen to innocent victims. As one victim of childhood abuse said, "Do you really expect me to believe in a loving, omnipotent God? Whatever God is like, I don't want anything to do with someone who let a little girl be battered and bruised and violated by her father and brother."

The struggles of childhood victims of abuse to reconcile their experience of violation and victimization sound hauntingly like those of survivors of concentration camps. "Where was God?" "Why did God allow this to happen?" "How can I integrate this experience into the rest of my life and go on living?" "How can I ever trust and be happy again?"

Instead of trivializing pain and glorifying suffering, we must gently walk with victims as they strive to make sense of their experience, as they struggle to live with woundedness, as they search for healing.

**6. *Christians must promptly forgive those who sin against them*.** Forgiveness will be explored more fully in chapter 7. But it is necessary to mention the necessity of prompt forgiveness as a sixth Christian teaching which may contribute to sexual abuse of children.

The Christian community has always placed a high premium on forgiveness. The psychological community in recent years has come to understand that, even from a nonspiritual perspective, the ability to forgive someone who has offended and hurt us is an important step toward our own healing and happiness.

Not only has the ability and willingness to forgive been held up as a primary Christian virtue, but emphasis has been placed on promptness. Those who find they can't quickly forgive someone who has offended them feel they have failed. They often fear God will not forgive their sins.

Many victims of sexual abuse tell of having their abusers come to them time and time again to ask forgiveness even while the abuse continued. One says,

> My dad would come into my room and fondle me at night. Before he'd even leave, he would demand that I forgive him. He said that if I ever told anyone, even when I was an adult, it meant that I hadn't really forgiven him. I would go to hell because God wouldn't forgive me.

As an adult, this survivor understands that her father's demands for forgiveness were a ploy to keep her quiet. Her strong belief in the Christian necessity of prompt forgiveness made her susceptible to this manipulative, deceptive tactic.

Other abusers are sincerely contrite about their behavior. Because they beg for forgiveness with obvious remorse, victims feel it would be vindictive and unchristlike to report the abuse to a nonoffending parent, teacher, police officer, or church person. Wanting to forgive with Christian graciousness, victims often respond with quick forgiveness.

By so doing they may deny offenders the possibility of being held accountable for their behavior and make it less likely offenders will get the help they need to truly change. By extending forgiveness without bringing the sinful behavior into the open, where it can be confronted and dealt with, the victim opens herself to possible revictimization. Particularly in the case of sexual abuse, it is appropriate to demand changed behavior as part of the process of forgiveness.

The above six religious beliefs must be honestly examined to understand how they may both explicitly and implicitly be related to abuse in Christian homes. Looking at our own sacred cows will be hard. It will be uncomfortable to look at ways in which some of our deepest beliefs may jeopardize the well-being of women and children. However, the cost of perpetuating a theology which may violate some of our most vulnerable people is great indeed. We dare no longer overlook that price.

## Chapter 6
# Pastoral Abuse

Some may wonder why a chapter on pastoral abuse appears in a book devoted primarily to sexual abuse within the family. With growing awareness of intrafamilial incestuous abuse has come awareness of another kind of incest among Christians—the sexual exploitation of parishioners by pastors.

Those of us working with people who have been abused by either a trusted family member or a trusted pastor see many parallels in contributing factors and resultant issues for victims. Similar fortresses of denial surround the problems of sexual abuse in both Christian homes and churches.

The church is frequently called the "family of God." Parishioners are likely to refer to their local congregation as "my church family." Jesus uses family terminology for the kingdom when he calls God "Father" and when he says, "Whoever does the will of God is my brother and sister and mother" (Mark: 3:35).

The operational structure of most congregations still resembles patriarchal families where positions of leadership, authority, and decision making tend to be held by men. Women tend to fill positions of childcare, nurture, and service. Like parents, pastors are often privy to intimate knowledge about parishioners.

And like children with parents, parishioners assume they can trust the pastor not to misuse or violate their trust and vulnerability. Tragically, just as in the biological family, power and trust are sometimes abused and betrayed in the church family.

Many find it unthinkable that someone called into a position of spiritual leadership would be capable of abusing parishioners. Yes, we acknowledge that "pastors are people" and face the same temptations as all of us. But we expect those whom we and God have called into spiritual leadership to have the spiritual resources and moral rectitude to resist such temptation.

Statistics show a different picture, however. *Christianity Today* conducted a poll to determine the extent of sexually inappropriate behavior among pastors. One question asked was, "Since you've been in local ministry, have you ever done anything with someone (not your spouse) that you feel was sexually inappropriate?" Twenty-three percent of the pastors answered "yes." Another question was, "Have you ever had sexual intercourse with someone other than your spouse since you've been in local-church ministry?" Twelve percent answered "yes." Of the 88 percent who answered "no," many indicated that maintaining sexual purity within their pastoral role had been very difficult (Muck, 1989).

Research conducted by Lebacqz and Barton (1991) found that 10 percent of pastors surveyed admitted they had become sexually involved with a parishioner. The true extent of pastoral abuse is unknown. Pastors are hesitant to confess such sin, victims are reluctant to talk about their abuse and congregations are anxious to sweep "rumors" or accusations of pastoral abuse under the pew.

The good news is that most pastors probably behave in sexually appropriate ways within the congregation. The bad news is that a significant number of pastors misuse their position and abuse parishioners. Later in this chapter we will explore the dire consequences of such behavior.

Just as with incestuous abuse in the family, there has been a great and successful conspiracy of silence regarding pastoral abuse. When the sexual misconduct of pastors and church leaders has been discovered, congregations, institutions, and denominations have generally tried to hush up victims, to discredit them, and to keep them isolated from each other.

A common response has been anger at the victim for besmirching the reputation of pastor and church. If the abusive leader or pastor is fired, the general pattern has been to maintain secrecy about the reason. Some abusive leaders have negotiated deals with their churches or institutions whereby the leader agrees to resign and leave his position if the institution promises never to tell why his employment was terminated.

Thus abusers can move from congregation to congregation and institution to institution without having to face their misconduct. They may never be forced to get the extensive therapy needed to change their behaviors. And adequate information about their inappropriate behavior may never be made known to those considering them for future employment or ministry in the church.

I am frequently asked if I think there is an increase in pastoral abuse. Since more energy has gone into trying to cover up abuse than into evaluating and rectifying the problem, there is no way to know the true frequency, now or in the past. My hunch is that the rate has probably always been about the same but that we are now hearing more about the problem.

Reports of sexual impurity in the lives of Jim Bakker and Jimmy Swaggart captivated the very medium—television—these men had manipulated to catapult themselves into positions of wealth and power. The public was eager to learn the next chapter in their sordid stories. The high media visibility of these men and their behaviors have made sexual immorality among famous preachers a hot topic of conversation.

A more significant factor making it appear pastoral abuse is increasing is willingness of victims to talk. For many generations victims had no forum in which to share their pain. They had no models of victims who had successfully gone to their churches with accounts of pastoral abuse and been believed. Instead they blamed themselves and suffered alone, in silence, and the rest of us never knew. Now more and more victims are finding the support and courage to tell their stories.

# A Victim's Story

Here is the story of Susan (not her real name).

I was delighted when our congregation hired Ron (not his real name). He was energetic and charismatic. He spoke in his candidating interview of his commitment to prayer and fasting, spiritual disciplines I had recently decided I needed to learn more about. He was middle-aged and married, with children. I was in my mid-twenties, single, and had never seriously dated.

Soon after his installation as our pastor, Ron announced from the pulpit that he was looking forward to getting to know us as a congregation and also individually. He invited any of us who wanted to talk to him privately to schedule an appointment with his secretary, which I soon did.

A few days later I went to the church for my appointment. I checked in with the secretary who buzzed the pastor. He came out, escorted me into his office, and closed the door. I never had a close relationship with my father and have never felt attractive to or comfortable around men. So I felt flattered when Ron warmly shook my hand, held it, and told me how delighted he was to have some time alone with me as he'd been noticing my "attentive, bright face" in the audience the past few Sundays.

We sat on a sofa in his office while he asked me lots of questions about myself. I soon found myself opening up to him, telling him things I'd never told a man before. When I told him about my strained relationship with my father, he put his arm around my shoulder and pulled me over against him.

He said, "Your father is the one who lost the most. Does he have any idea what a special girl you are? I can tell you will become a special gift to me."

I was embarrassed by his comment because it felt very personal, given the short time we'd known each other. Because I was embarrassed, I tried to move the conversation to something less personal. I told him I hoped he could teach me how to pray more meaningfully.

He said he'd be glad to and told me we could set up a weekly appointment if I'd like. He asked me to keep a daily journal of my activities and thoughts. I was to record my dreams so he could help me interpret them and hear what God was saying to me through my dreams—which were a form of prayer, he explained.

Then his secretary buzzed him and said his next appointment

was waiting, so I prepared to leave. Ron took my hands in his, squeezed them, and said he could already tell this friendship was going to be something special for both of us. As he told me good-bye, he still held my hands and looked intently into my eyes. I remember pulling my hands away because they were shaking and I didn't want him to know how my body was responding.

That night, when I began journaling, I realized that I couldn't be honest about my feelings because it would be too embarrassing for him to know how I had responded to his physical and emotional closeness during the counseling session.

That night I had a dream that he and I were walking together through an orchard on a beautiful summer day. We were holding hands. I was too embarrassed to let him know about that dream so I lied and recorded the next morning that I'd had no dreams. For the rest of the week, I carefully monitored everything I put in my journal.

At our second counseling session, he told me he was disappointed in the shallowness of my journal. He said he believed I was blocking. What was I trying to hide from him? He told me I could never expect to grow spiritually if I wasn't willing to be totally open and honest with him.

He said his pastoral intuition told him I was repressing a very important part of my God-created personality—my sexuality—and that was probably stunting my growth in all areas of my life.

Then he began to ask how I handled my sexuality. Was I celibate? Had I ever been sexually involved with a man? With a woman? Did I masturbate? Did I ever watch dirty movies? Did I fantasize? Had I fantasized about him during the week?

He told me not to be ashamed of being honest with him because all these things were normal and to be expected. He also said that because I had been emotionally wounded by my earthly father, I could never have a close relationship with my heavenly Father unless I developed a close relationship with a man. As my pastor, he suggested, he would be a safe man to be close to. He added that he and his wife had not been emotionally or sexually close for several years and our friendship would be "good for both of us."

Again I felt uneasy with the direction the conversation was going. But I chalked up my anxiety to lack of experience with men. After all, hadn't several of my friends accused me of being a prude when it came to guys? And wasn't this man my pastor? Surely he wouldn't suggest anything inappropriate.

Over the next several weeks our conversations were more and

more about sexual issues and infrequently about spiritual matters —except for his reminding me you couldn't separate sexuality from spirituality. "Hang-ups in one area cause hang-ups in the other."

There was more and more physical contact and the good-bye hand squeezes soon turned into full-bodied good-bye hugs. One day he gave me a deep, long kiss as he hugged me good-bye. I told him that I didn't feel comfortable kissing another woman's husband.

He assured me it wasn't "that kind of kiss." If it wasn't, my body didn't know, because I found myself feeling light-headed after the kiss. I don't think his body knew it either because I felt his erect penis against my leg as he kissed me.

When I left his office, I was ashamed to walk by his secretary because I was afraid she could tell by looking at me that I was sexually excited. So I left through a side door.

The following Sunday I considered not going to church. I dreaded having to face his wife and children because I felt I had betrayed them. Because I had a class to teach, I did go. But during the worship service I sat in the back of the auditorium where Ron couldn't see me while he preached and from where I could exit quickly. The next day I called the church secretary and canceled my weekly counseling appointment with Ron.

My roommate works the night shift at the local hospital. Ron knew this. Tuesday evening he showed up at our apartment and asked if he could come in. I told him I really didn't think he should; I asked him to go away.

He reminded me that he was my pastor, after all. He just wanted to talk. I thought perhaps he had come to apologize for the direction our counseling sessions had taken and for his physical forwardness with me. So I let him come in.

He asked me to sit beside him on the sofa. He told me how hurt and disappointed he was that I had canceled our counseling appointment. He believed we were just on the brink of getting into some very important stuff in my spiritual journey.

I told him I didn't want to continue counseling with him anymore because I didn't feel comfortable with the relationship. It no longer felt like a pastoral relationship and I was scared.

He told me again what he had often said before: I had sexual hang-ups common to "old maids." To get near God I'd have to get over them. "Believe me, I've worked with lots of other women in your situation; I know what I'm talking about."

Then he added, "But you're not just another counselee; you're very special to God and to me. I think I'm in love with you."

I began crying. The tears were a mixture of fear and tenderness for I had never been told by a man that he loved me. Here was my handsome pastor saying these romantic things to me. Part of me wanted to believe that if he felt comfortable saying them it must be all right and his views must be true. But deep down I knew some usual pastoral boundary had been crossed.

Now he put his arms around me and pulled me nearer him and tried to wipe away my tears. I tried to pull away and get up.

Something in him seemed to snap when I physically pulled away. He started yelling at me. "Oh, no, you don't—you've led me on this far and you're not going to back down now!" He shoved me down on the sofa, put his knee in my stomach, and started grabbing my breasts. He kissed me and wildly rubbed his genitals against my body.

I wasn't strong enough to shove him off. Even though I was crying and struggling, he continued until he was finished.

Then he got up and stomped out the door yelling, "If you think you can ruin me, you are wrong. Nobody will believe a sex-starved old maid like you if you ever try to tell anyone about this! You're the one who will suffer!"

Regrettably, Ron was right. Susan never returned to worship with her congregation. Instead she called the congregational chairperson, resigned her teaching duties, and asked to have her church membership terminated. Asked why she was leaving, she said, "Because of personal problems."

Susan became severely depressed and was put on antidepressant medication. The doctor prescribing the medication told her he would not continue prescribing it unless she went into therapy. Because she had never told anyone about the abuse, not even her roommate, she found it frightening to tell her story to the therapist. She felt deep shame and blamed herself for being so naive, so needy, so inexperienced. She felt abandoned by God and her church.

Through therapy, healing began. Susan started to understand that instead of having been stupid she had been victimized and that her abuse had not only been sexual. Perhaps more damaging, she had experienced the results of profound abuse of power and betrayal of trust by someone she considered to represent God's face.

As she grew stronger, she decided she needed to tell someone in the congregation what had happened. When she felt ready, Susan wrote her story and delivered it to a church elder. She asked him to read and share it with the other elders. She requested that they decide what procedures to follow to confront Pastor Ron. She asked that they let her know of the process. She agreed to cooperate in any way possible because she was concerned that other women were being victimized.

Several hours after she delivered her written story to the elder, Susan received a call from him. The elder was disturbed that she would say such vicious things about Pastor Ron. Susan clearly needed a boyfriend, the elder said, but "don't go after the preacher."

She was devastated by his response but insisted that he share the letter with the other elders. The following week another elder called to tell her that as a board having spiritual authority over her, they were informing her she could not mention this to anyone ever again. Susan reminded them she had asked that her church membership letter be returned to her. They said that until she joined another church, she remained under their spiritual authority.

Several months later, Susan ran into another young woman who mentioned that she no longer went to Ron's church. As they began talking, they discovered both had been abused by Pastor Ron. They also shared similar aftereffects of depression and a sense of betrayal and abandonment by God and their congregation.

After meeting together for several weeks to share their pain, they wrote a letter telling of their experiences with Ron and asked denominational leaders to make sure other women weren't victimized.

They did receive a response. They were told these matters should be handled at the congregational level. The local board of elders had been urged to investigate the matter.

It appears no further steps have been taken to investigate the allegations against Pastor Ron. No expression of support or apology has come from the church or the denomination to these victims. No restitution has been offered.

The two known victims remain detached from their previous church and from all churches because of their sense of betrayal and abandonment by the institutional church. They both are in therapy. They continue to battle depression and feelings of abandonment, rage, and despair. Ron, however, continues on as senior pastor.

## Resultant Spiritual and Emotional Damage for Victims

The story of Susan shares many things in common with accounts of other victims of pastoral sexual abuse. Underlying themes center around betrayal of trust and abuse of power.

Most people place great trust in their pastor. Even if she has experienced abuse from other men in her life, a woman generally assumes that the pastor is different. He can be trusted to have her best interests at heart and to keep her safe. Most women assume they don't need to maintain their usual vigilance when with their pastor; they may instead trust him to maintain appropriate boundaries. The resulting relaxation of usual boundary defenses makes women even more vulnerable and the professional even more powerful than in most male-female relationships.

Women have been socialized to comply with the demands of men in positions of authority. Girls learn at an early age that to resist the demands of powerful men may invite negative outcomes for them. This, coupled with the high level of trust most women bring into a relationship with a pastor, makes it hard for women to comprehend and believe a pastor may be engaging in inappropriate behavior. "I assumed that if he was doing those things to me it must be all right." "Wasn't this man my pastor? Surely he wouldn't suggest anything that wasn't proper."

An impaired ability to trust becomes an ongoing issue for victims of pastoral abuse. Because many see the pastor as mediator between God and the congregation, the violation of trust has even more damaging effects than if abuser had been a doctor, boss, or some other male authority figure in an abused woman's life.

Because the pastor is often seen as a spiritual mentor and model, the spiritual damage and violation is profound when mentor also becomes sexual abuser. Later we will explore further the deep connection between sexuality and spirituality. Woundedness in one area will inevitably result in woundedness in the other. On this, Pastor Ron was right.

Because the counseling relationship often is terminated abruptly after sexual abuse occurs, deep feelings of abandonment and disorganization may follow for the victim. Since the counseling process has been prematurely terminated, many unresolved therapeutic issues remain.

Since she was unable to foresee the direction her relationship with the pastor was taking, or was unable to change the dynamics of the relationship, the abused woman may doubt her own sense of reality and personal effectiveness. The guilt, shame, and humiliation she may feel often prevent her from talking to another counselor or pastor about the abuse. Because churches historically have been ineffective confronting situations of pastoral abuse, and awkward in reaching out to victims, the victims' sense is that they have been abandoned, not only by the pastor and God, but also by their congregation.

Many times victims are blamed by congregations for "destroying a good man." Often it is easier for churches to focus frustration on victims and blame them than to acknowledge that a pastor has sinned and flagrantly abused his position. Numerous victims have told of threats against them and their reputation if they did not retract their accusations. Some have told of official silencing, of being ordered by denominational authorities never to talk again about their abuse.

Some victims have told of blatant lies spread about the victim's morality and integrity in an attempt to undermine accusations. When the victim loves the church, yet wants to see justice done and further victims spared, these directives place her in a double bind: she cannot obey both the church she loves and also her inner conscience, which demands that she work to prevent further victimization of innocent people.

A disturbing phenomenon has been observed in instances where women have brought accusations of sexual abuse against a respected pastor or leader. Other women may express more outrage against the accusers than do men.

Yes, men also frequently respond in anger to the victim. It may frighten some men to realize that the silence on which abusers could count for so many years is breaking. Male privilege may seem threatened. It may disturb some that "uppity women can't be counted on to know their place and keep their mouths shut." "If it happened to one of those men, it could happen to me." Women's willingness to charge pastors publicly with abuse may be disturbing, annoying, and disgusting for other men.

For women, however, the fallout of such accusations may seem life threatening. When working as a mediator for a conciliation service, I had opportunity to interview numerous women who had expressed anger at sister members who brought sexual abuse charges against a pastor in their conservative denomination.

Several women said that because men hold most of the power in church, home, and the world, women's very survival depends on maintaining good relations with men. Otherwise men may not share what women need to survive. "If women go around making men too angry, they may abandon us. Then we and our children will die."

It is no wonder victims of pastoral abuse are considered at increased risk of suicide. Suicidal feelings may come from a variety of sources, including the sense of abandonment by other church sisters and the suppressed rage victims may feel but are unable to express. Because they have no prescribed forum for expressing their anger against the abusive pastor, the intense feelings may turn inward and become a self-destructive pool of rage.

If victims' pleas to get the church they love and respect to discipline the abusive pastor are disregarded, profound hopelessness may set in. Sometimes when pastor and church turn their backs, the victim is left with a sense of terrifying abandonment. When abuse survivors feel deserted and betrayed by the pastor, the church, and God, it is no wonder their despair sometimes finds tragic, poignant expression in suicide.

The serious, long-term spiritual and emotional scars of pastoral abuse have often been minimized by denominations and church leaders. Attention instead has focused on damage to a pastor's career and marriage and the detrimental implications for church growth.

A blatant example of downplaying abuse is found in a book on pastoral abuse by a well-known Christian author (LaHaye, 1990). In a chapter on "The High Cost of Ministerial Infidelity," the author explores the cost for the minister, his career, his marriage, his wife, his family, the church, Christianity, and the lost. Flagrantly missing from this chapter and from the entire book is an exploration of the damage done to the pastor's victim, referred to throughout the book as "the other woman." Pastoral sexual abuse is often but incorrectly seen as mere adulterous behavior between two consenting people. Rarely is this an accurate or helpful conceptual framework.

Now let's turn to the complex task of trying to understand the dynamics of pastoral abuse. It may be easy to believe that remote showmen like Swaggart and Bakker fall into sexual temptation. But it is harder for most people to imagine that their own decent pastor could ever cross appropriate sexual boundaries with church members. Yet more and more congregations are being forced to acknowledge that their pastors have committed sexual violations in the congregation. Why and how does this happen?

## Imbalance of Power

Peter Rutter (1989) accurately observes that sexual violation in a professional relationship of trust is a widespread problem that reenacts the broader cultural imbalance of power between men and women. In our society men have more power in general. They have more earning power, more social and physical power, and more political power.

For example, a college-educated woman between ages eighteen and twenty-four earns, on average, ninety-two cents for every dollar earned by a man in the same age and education category. Throughout her working life, her earnings drop steadily in comparison to her male counterpart. By the time she is between ages fifty-five and sixty-four, the average woman is making just fifty-four cents for every dollar earned by men with similar education.

Studies have also shown that the ideas of men are given more serious attention and consideration than those of women in social, educational, religious, and work settings. Men are usually physically larger and stronger than women. The gender imbalance of political power is reflected in the fact that of one hundred United States senators, only a handful are women.

No matter how low his level of self-esteem or personal self-confidence, the male pastor embodies the generalized power of men as a class in our sexist society. In addition, the pastor's religious role carries with it significant inherent power and authority. The pastor is considered by many to be God's representative and a mediator between the congregation and God. Because of the power advantage the male pastor has as a man, plus the specific power of his pastoral position, he has, with perhaps very rare exceptions, significantly more power than any woman in his congregation.

Because of his position and authority, a pastor may have immediate and intimate access to people. He may show up at parishioners' homes or work places at any time of the day or night under the guise of a "pastoral visit." Few openly question the appropriateness of a pastor's visitation patterns. Fewer still ever turn the pastor away if he shows up on their doorstep unannounced and unwanted. Because of his position and authority, we grant the pastor liberties of entry into our lives we don't grant others.

A pastor sometimes has access to information rarely shared with another human being. Because spirituality and spiritual questions come from our very core, a pastor may have knowledge about people no one else has. Because this level of intimate sharing is not reciprocal, power between a male pastor and female parishioner is rarely equal.

Women have been socialized to view their bodies as their best bargaining chip in life, their source of power. Thus they become vulnerable to physical advances made toward them by males in authority. Because many women feel powerless, and because they are trained to accept the challenging of sexual boundaries by men as normal, women often cannot resist the advances of someone as powerful as a male pastor.

The imbalance of power between men and women has become eroticized in our culture. Many persons find male power and female powerlessness sexually arousing. In general, men are sexually attracted to females who are younger, smaller, and less powerful than themselves. Women tend to be attracted to males who are older, larger, and more powerful. Male clergy have a great imbalance of power over their congregations which are often predominately women, therefore, the stage is set for a sexually inappropriate expression of this power differential.

Pastors often feel overworked, underpaid, and devalued. Thus they may find it difficult to understand the notion of pastoral power, since they personally may feel ineffective and weak.

Particularly young, inexperienced pastors struggle with insecurities about their roles and may feel much more powerless than powerful in their new position. Though they remain accountable for their behavior, such pastors may misuse their power before fully realizing they have it. This difference between fledgling and mature abusers deserves acknowledgment.

Yet all pastors must be confronted with the fact that inability to acknowledge the special power privilege of their position is dangerous. Pastors are more susceptible to abusing precisely the power that they have difficulty acknowledging.

## The Blurry Boundary Between Sexuality and Spirituality

Another factor contributing to the occurrence of sexual involvement between pastor and parishioners is the often blurry boundary between human sexuality and spirituality. Carl Jung observed that when people came to him with sexual questions they in fact turned out to be spiritual questions. When people came with spiritual questions they invariably turned out to be sexual in nature. Psychologists often observe that spiritual and sexual desires are so closely intertwined that when one is aroused so too is the other.

The human quest for God often taps into an energy which feels similar to sexual passion. Our longing for intimacy with the divine often reminds us of our longing for deep intimacy with another human being. One woman reflects this relationship when she says, "Times of fasting and prayer for me often result in a feeling of being washed away in one gigantic orgasmic wave of loving God and being loved by God."

Many people describe spiritual longing in words that sound sexual. "I place so much emphasis on prayer in my life because I have a pervasive desire to experience intimacy and union with God." Some report actual feelings and physiological indications of sexual arousal during times of deep prayer as their embodied selves long passionately for God.

Likewise, many people describe experiences of sexual intimacy in spiritual vocabulary. "I have never felt closer to God than those times when my husband and I are sexually synchronized and can give and take passionate pleasure without concern for the ordinary demands of children, jobs, and responsibilities. At its best, our lovemaking has an almost numinous quality about it," says one woman.

In both sexual and spiritual experiences, humans lower their defenses and experience greater vulnerability. Deep spiritual renewal and true sexual pleasure both require a letting go of control and an abandonment to the experience. Personal ego boundaries become less defined. We experience a sense of union with something greater than ourselves both in times of worship and in times of sexual intimacy.

Because the energies of human spirituality and sexuality are similar in some ways, working with a parishioner on spiritual issues in an intimate setting such as the pastor's office may trigger sexual feelings in both the pastor and the pastored. As the professional, it is the pastor's responsibility to assure that those feelings are not acted on. When people come to the pastor for counseling, they should be able to assume that even though their defenses are down (a necessary and important step in the counseling process), the pastor will keep them safe and set appropriate boundaries.

Ours is a culture which has taught women it is their responsibility to set sexual boundaries and limits, no matter what the nature of the particular female-male relationship. Men have been taught it is part of the manly role to push and challenge those limits and boundaries. In spite of these cultural standards, in the pastoral relationship it must be clearly understood that the responsibility for maintaining appropriate sexual boundaries rests with the pastor.

## Structural and Emotional Factors of the Pastorate

To better understand how some pastors come to sexually violate and abuse the trust and authority placed in them, we now look at certain structural and emotional factors operating within the pastorate and the congregation.

In our culture there appears to be something erotically charged about relationships where men hold power and women place their trust and hope in men. As was mentioned earlier, ours is a culture which finds men's power and women's powerlessness sexy.

When women open up the most intimate aspects of their psychological, emotional, and spiritual selves to a man, it seems to eroticize the relationship (Rutter, 1989). Men tend to find it sexually affirming and exciting to have women dependent on them for support, comfort, and guidance. This is the very role many pastors play in the lives of many women in the congregation.

The work setting of the pastor lends itself to the possibility of acting out eroticized feelings which may have developed between pastor and parishioner. Much pastoral counseling is done in the pastor's office with the door closed. In many smaller churches the pastor often is the only person in the church building during most of the week. It is considered appropriate and often desirable for pastors to visit members in the hospital or their homes. Likewise, it is considered appropriate to welcome a pastor doing church visitation into the home.

For the pastor tempted to become sexually involved with a member, there are many opportunities and places to act out the desire without being noticed or raising suspicions. Because of confidentiality issues, pastors' spouses are used to vague responses when they ask, "Who did you see today?" or "What were you doing tonight?"

Most professional counselors work under a supervisor with whom they periodically review cases and discuss issues such as transference (strong feelings the counselee may develop toward the counselor) and countertransference (strong feelings the counselor may develop toward the counselee). Most pastors, however, schedule and see counselees with total autonomy and independence. Rare is the congregation which provides regular supervision and feedback for a pastor's counseling ministry and involvement. Few church boards know specifically how a pastor spends his time and fewer know much about his counseling involvements. Pastoral counseling accountability and supervision is flagrantly missing from most congregational structures.

The intimate and private nature of the pastor's counseling involvement with members, the erotic component of powerful male and powerless female relationships, and the lack of well-defined mechanisms of supervision and accountability create an atmosphere where sexual involvement becomes possible. It is perhaps a tribute to the spiritual character and moral strength of most pastors that the incidence of pastoral abuse isn't higher.

There are numerous emotional hazards of ministry which appear to contribute to pastoral susceptibility to abuse sexually. While there is much prestige, power, and authority inherent in a pastor's position, these very things can contribute to a sense of isolation from other members in the congregation.

It's hard to be "one of the guys" when you are the pastor. Even if you are playing volleyball at the church picnic or caroling at the retirement center, you are still and foremost the pastor and people expect you to act in ways consistent with that role. Church members likewise may monitor their behavior when the pastor is near for fear he may be assessing their spirituality. Such factors may cause the pastor to feel emotionally isolated and lonely within the congregation.

Many pastors find congregations expect the pastor to be an expert teacher, preacher, counselor, public relations director, fundraiser and administrator. Because most people who enter the ministry are hardworking and devoted, unrealistic job expectations may cause them to work and work, yet feel they never get caught up. The result is pastoral stress and burnout. Prolonged stress is an important factor in the development of alcoholism, drug abuse, overeating and other addictions, depression, anxiety, heart attacks, and cancer. In addition, prolonged stress is suspected of contributing to "carnaling out"—as pastors sometimes call inappropriate sexual behaviors.

Few churches have devised mechanisms for effectively providing emotional support for the pastor. Thus he often has no one to whom he can turn to share spiritual doubts, loneliness, and temptations. Some pastors tell of finding support and loving companionship from clergy in other churches. Unfortunately, most pastors are overworked and consider such fraternizing a luxury which can be indulged in only "when all the work is done."

The workaholic devotion many pastors give to their ministry makes good spiritual companionship difficult to build into their lives; it also contributes to emotional alienation from spouses. When pastors do not have regular, intimate support and opportunities for deep sharing with Christian friends, they are more likely to turn to female counselees or woman parishioners for understanding and affection. In such situations, pastors run a high risk of sexualizing a relationship from which they may really want emotional support and affirmation.

## Personal Qualities of Some Ministers

What are common personal histories and personality characteristics of people attracted to the ministry? How do such factors contribute to pastoral abuse?

Many people choose to become pastors for healthy, admirable reasons. Even pastors who later discover that career choice motivations were influenced by less noble unconscious factors often face their brokenness, acknowledge their shadows, and serve their congregations in healthy, wholesome, redemptive ways.

A high percentage of people in the helping professions (counseling, social work, nursing, psychiatry, ministry, for example) come from dysfunctional childhood homes. Choosing such professions may be an unconscious attempt to gain understanding and relief from personal brokenness and pain. What is wanted is the care and love denied in childhood. But instead of facing personal neediness and learning how to ask for care, these needy people become professional caretakers of others.

Studies of pastors do reflect this trend; many pastors report having had unhappy childhoods. Characteristics of adult children who came from emotionally unhealthy homes include tendency to workaholism and insensitivity to personal emotional needs. Such qualities may influence a pastor to become over-extended emotionally and physically. They may make him susceptible to high stress and burnout. Sexual acting out has been identified as one way of relieving stress and trying to inject new energy into a life headed for burnout.

As has been suggested, many pastors have an intense desire and need to care for others and make them happy. Many enter the ministry to get the love and affirmation they so desperately craved but didn't get as children. The congregation then becomes a kind of surrogate parent, and the minister hopes to be cherished and valued in ways he longed for as a child.

Unfortunately, this is an unrealistic expectation for a congregation to fulfill. In his disappointment at not having these needs met by the congregation, the pastor may instead turn to a nurturing, affirming individual parishioner. Because of socialization, the male pastor will most likely look to a woman to find this emotional support. Longing for deep affirmation and intimacy, the pastor may be vulnerable to crossing appropriate emotional boundaries with his confidante. Because of the male tendency to genitalize feelings, he may find himself sexually aroused by his female friend and be tempted to sexualize the relationship.

Certain personality styles are commonly found among pastors. The Enneagram is an ancient tool used by spiritual directors to help people understand their personality style and personal compulsions. Using Enneagram terminology (Rohr and Ebert, 1991), number two types are attracted to the ministry in large numbers. This should not be surprising since twos are the caretakers, the "I need to be needed," the "I am helpful" people. Twos are warm people comfortable with physical touch. They easily reach out to others and quickly form friendships. Service is important to twos, and they tend to be generous with their time and possessions.

While aspects of the *perceived* ministerial role may draw twos into pastoral training, the *reality* of the minister's job may frustrate and emotionally starve type two pastors. Because they are prone to depression when emotional needs aren't met, twos may find the actual pastoral role stifling to their well-being. If they feel unappreciated, twos may become resentful, bitter, and manipulative. When the demands of the ministerial role (many of which tend to isolate the pastor from other people) materialize, type two pastors may sink into depression. Because twos are better at meeting other people's needs than facing their own neediness, they may emotionally disintegrate before they understand how depleted are their spiritual and emotional reservoirs.

Twos get energized again by moving toward people, by caring for others and becoming close to them—sometimes in manipulative ways. Because women are seen as more likely to offer close companionship and emotional relatedness than men, the type two pastor will likely look to women in the congregation for the relationships he needs. Since twos are not very good at understanding their own neediness, the pastor's deep needs for affirmation and relatedness may become sexualized.

Research using the Myers-Briggs Type Indicator has found that 69 percent of ministers are feeling-oriented types and 44 percent are both feeling and intuition oriented (Oswald and Kroeger, 1988). Only 12 percent of the general population is both feeling and intuition oriented. The positive attributes for ministry of an intuitive and feeling personality style are empathy, charisma, and deep capacity for care. Pastoral candidates often have an advantage if they are intuitive-feeling types, for they come across as the classic good pastor—warm, loving, kind, and empathetic.

On the other hand, intuitive feeling types tend to foster relationships where they can rescue others and people are dependent on them. They also need constant affirmation and personal expressions of appreciation. They handle criticism less well than other types. Most congregations are not good at consistently supporting and affirming the pastor.

Since the pastorate attracts many workaholics who may also be intuitive-feeling types, there are many ministers who may work harder and harder in a futile attempt to get the affirmation they crave from the congregation. This, coupled with the intuitive feeling persons' general willingness to make great personal sacrifices for what they believe in, sets up pastors for high levels of frustration and stress—both correlated with pastoral sexual abuse.

One final personality category must be considered in discussing pastoral abuse and personality factors. This is the blatant, sociopathic sex offender who chooses the ministry because he knows it will give him access to vulnerable victims for his perverse sexual pleasure. This type of offender appears to be found more often in youth ministries. This may be due to the fact that youth ministers are not always required to undergo the extensive academic training and internship of the regular pastorate. Many churches call on volunteer youth ministers loved for their basic "good guy" qualities.

But most perpetrators of pastoral abuse did not enter the ministry intending to violate their sacred trust and position. Instead, they succumbed to an interaction of factors related to the imbalance of power, the structural and emotional issues inherent in ministry, and their own personal characteristics and moral qualities. However, spiritual and emotional damage to victims does not correlate with pastoral intentions. Whether a pastor came into ministry because it offered opportunities to abuse vulnerable people or came with noble intentions but "fell" into abuse, the implications for victims are devastating and long lasting.

## Guidelines for Pastors

This section offers suggestions for male pastors who want to function in healthy, nonabusive ways within the congregation.

**1. *Be honest about your power*.** Acknowledge that as a man in a patriarchal culture you have more power in general than women. You have more economic power, more political power, and more social power. Your pastoral position gives you additional role-specific authority and power. Commit yourself never to abuse that power.

**2.** *Be honest about your susceptibility.* Even though your pastoral role places you on a spiritual pedestal, acknowledge your own susceptibility to inappropriate sexual thoughts and behavior. Face and confess the seductiveness of authority and power. The myth of pastoral invulnerability makes ministers susceptible to self-deception and flagrant sin.

**3.** *Face your woundedness.* Find the courage and resources to understand and face the brokenness and pain you carry from childhood. Do everything possible to be healed. Beware of wanting to find a female within the congregation to nurture you and heal your pain. Learn to identify and care for your emotional needs in appropriate ways.

**4.** *Nurture your own spirituality.* Don't let your responsibility for the congregation's spiritual well-being distract you from the need to cultivate your own spiritual life. Take the time and energy necessary to practice spiritual disciplines which enrich and nurture your inner life.

**5.** *Tend your personal life and develop intimate friendships with other men.* Take time to develop outside interests and friendships. If you are married, make your relationship with your spouse a top priority. Build communication, romance, and fun into your intimate relationship and stay sensitive to its health and vitality. Learn to relate to other men in deep friendship and emotional intimacy.

**6.** *Be aware of sexual energy within the congregation.* Because spiritual and sexual desires are so closely related, you cannot have one without the other. Be honest about this relationship. When denied and repressed, sexual energy within the church becomes dangerous and destructive.

**7.** *Develop counseling guidelines and safeguards.* Consider taking along a friend or spouse when making pastoral visits. Limit yourself to doing short-term counseling. It may not be appropriate or wise for a male pastor to undertake counseling with a female on sexual or other deeply personal matters.

Ask your church board to consider hiring a woman pastoral counselor to join the staff. Find a professional counselor to provide supervision and feedback for your counseling ministry. Get the training you require to be aware of and appropriately manage issues of transference and countertransference

**8. Be sensitive to danger signs.** Know what the indicators are of possible movement toward an inappropriate relationship. Beware of frequent thoughts about a parishioner, of sexual fantasies and tendencies to want to spend more time with her. Beware of comparing her to your wife. Watch yourself for physical sensations of sexual arousal when you are with her or think about her. Watch for tendencies to turn conversations into talk about us or about sexual matters. Watch your dreams.

**9. Develop a mechanism for accountability and mentorship.** Find another Christian brother or pastor with whom you can meet regularly in honesty and transparency. Develop a relationship of spiritual mentorship with a spiritually mature man and commit yourself to being accountable to him. Share with him your temptations and acknowledge your susceptibility to abuse.

**10. Learn to relate to women in healthy ways.** Commit yourself to developing wholesome, nonsexual relationships with women. Learn how to have mutual, nonexploitive relationships with women where respect is mutual and power is shared.

## Chapter 7

# Repentance, Restitution, Forgiveness, and Reconciliation

With her toddler daughter balanced on one hip, and a cup of tea in her hand, the young mother shuffled to the front porch to gather the just-delivered mail. Still holding her child, she sat at the kitchen table to make two piles—items to be tossed immediately and those needing further attention.

In the midst of her mindless sorting, she came to an envelope addressed in handwriting that made her gasp. Although she had had no contact with either parent for over eight years, she recognized the slanted penmanship as her father's.

The woman's immediate sobs frightened the little girl, who asked, "Mommy have ouchy?"

After assuring her child that "mommy will be fine," she ran to her bedroom, fell onto the bed, and let long-suppressed waves of tears roll through her. Later she opened the crumpled letter which she had clenched in her fist and read,

This letter will probably come as a big surprise since we've not seen each other or had any communication for so long. I know you have been very angry at me for those things I used to do to you at night when you were a little girl. You're probably specially angry at me for saying I'd kill you if you ever told anyone about it. I'm thankful you didn't tell your mom and hope you haven't told anyone else.

I didn't know any better back then. I just became a real Christian several months ago. Since then I've been having lots of depression, and my minister asked me if I have any unconfessed sin. What I did to you is all I can think of, so I'm asking you to forgive me. I'd like to get to know my granddaughters so hope you'll plan a trip home sometime soon.

Don't say anything about this to Mom, because she doesn't know anything about what happened back then and she doesn't know about this letter. I hope your life has gone all right and that you'll forgive me. Write back as soon as possible. Love, Dad

One of the most complicated issues for victims of sexual abuse is forgiveness of and reconciliation with their abusers. Victims long to be free from the heavy burdens and darkness they carry inside their hearts. They dream of having relationships with their fathers, brothers, and grandfathers that are like those of nonabused friends. They would do almost anything to replace the fear and shame which permeate their childhood memories with normal, happy feelings. They wonder if forgiving would make this all possible. Whether or not it would make them happier, survivors know that as Christians they have no choice but to forgive their abusers. They may not be great biblical scholars, but they know Christians forgive.

Churches do teach that forgiveness of those who sin against us is a prerequisite for experiencing God's forgiveness and living a joyful Christian life. Not only have we learned we must forgive and be reconciled to those who trespass against us—but we must do it promptly.

In general, the responsibility for reconciliation between perpetrator and victim of sexual abuse has been placed on the victim. It has been assumed and communicated by many pastors and laypeople that if she will forgive her abuser and cast off bitter feelings, the relationship can be restored. While survivors of sexual abuse report varied responses from Christians with whom they share stories of victimization, a consistent concern has been to assess whether the victim has "really forgiven" the abuser.

Sadly, many victims report feeling reprimanded by Christian professionals for their inability to promptly forgive and forget. "When my pastor learned that the abuse had ended twenty-seven years ago, he said, 'Only a bitter, self-pitying woman would even remember these things after all those years.' " The pastor's response caused this woman to feel even more self-hatred and self-condemnation. She left the pastor's office with an overwhelming but familiar sense that she was guilty and evil. She attempted suicide that evening.

Reconciliation between victims and their offenders is surely an important and desirable goal, particularly when both are believers and members of the same congregation. As long as the relationship remains broken, not only are the key participants' lives affected, but also those of their families, the congregation, and the broader Christian community.

Thus, victims and offenders should be encouraged to work toward restored relationship. But reconciliation must be seen in the context of a longer, often difficult process which involves repentance, restitution, forgiveness—*then* reconciliation.

## Repentance

Reconciliation and restoration of a violated relationship cannot happen without true repentance by the offender. A truce may be called where the parties relate to each other on a superficial level without repentance, but that is not reconciliation.

The New Testament term for repentance is *metanoia,* which refers to a complete change of mind. Occurring almost synonymously with repentance in the Bible is a turning away from sin and toward God. Profound grief and deep sorrow for sin are a frequent accompaniment.

Because the church has long been uncomfortable talking about anything sexual, it has been particularly uncomfortable walking with people guilty of sexual sins through the long, hard steps of responsible repentance. Instead there has been a tendency to quickly forgive and offer "cheap grace," in Dietrich Bonhoeffer's terminology.

While it may be easier and more comfortable to accept the quick and easy apology of an offender, by so doing we cheat him of the opportunity truly to repent and experience God's forgiveness and grace. To accept an offender's cavalier apology "is a disrespectful disregard for what his soul is capable of offering through true repentance" (Allender, 1990, p. 239). Forgiveness without repentance may make the community feel better, but it is not a healing experience, either for victim or perpetrator.

Repentance is more than saying, "I'm sorry" or even "I'm sorry and I'll never do it again." Repentance involves admitting sin and looking unflinchingly at the awfulness of what has been done. It means feeling deep grief for the pain caused another. Depression and suicidal thoughts sometimes accompany this stage. Being in the presence of one who is sincerely contrite and repentant for sinfulness is an awesome experience, often accompanied by gut-wrenching sobs and heartfelt moans. True repentance is bound to hurt because it involves the bitter realization of inner wretchedness. Because of the agony of this step, the offender needs the support and love of Christian friends or a pastor.

After the offender has felt his own pain, he must be willing to acknowledge and feel the pain he has caused his victim. It isn't enough to admit intellectually that the abuse was terrible. He must come to the point where he can feel the victim's pain. This may involve long hours of listening to the victim talk about the effects of the abuse on her life. It may require reading the stories of other victims, or talking to a therapist about the ongoing effects of victimization.

Repentance means that the perpetrator must take the necessary steps to assure that his abusive behavior will never happen again. For some it will mean submitting to church discipline and working with a group of believers who hold the abuser in loving, firm accountability. For many repentance will include long, intensive psychotherapy to understand the roots of the abuse and learn ways of controlling inappropriate impulses.

For some abusers repentance may entail working with the legal system and getting appropriate treatment. For some it will mean facing addictive behavioral patterns and making a lifelong commitment to being in a Twelve Step or similar support group. For most abusers repentance will involve a complex unraveling of attitudes about men and women, about authority and submission, and a commitment to learn healthier patterns of relating to women and children. Sadly, congregations must acknowledge that because repentance is such a difficult step, for some offenders true repentance may never happen.

## Restitution

True repentance involves desire to make amends for sin and willingness to bear the consequences of the abuse. Anything else is not true repentance. There is nothing that can be done for or given to a victim of sexual abuse to make up for the pain and multiple losses she has suffered. Some form of restitution, however, may be an important step in the repentance and forgiveness process. Acts or gifts of symbolic reparation communicate that the offender is responsible for the sin of abuse and acknowledges to perpetrator, victim, and the community that a severe injury was done.

Victims and offenders usually need an outside person or group to help them choose an appropriate restitution plan. Restitution should require a sacrifice on the part of the offender and should benefit the victim. Sometimes an offender is asked to make a financial payment for the victim's therapy costs or for hospitalization resulting from depression. Sometimes he is asked to make a donation to organizations which treat victims of sexual or domestic violence.

One victim of pastoral abuse asked that the abuser donate money to financially assist women abused by church leaders to come together for support and sharing of personal stories of healing. One woman asked her father to pay for the cost of cosmetic surgery so she could have the scars of repeated suicide attempts removed from her wrists.

One little girl asked that her abusive older brother spend one hour each day riding bicycle with her or reading to her when he would have preferred playing Nintendo or hanging out with his buddies. He was also required to start a bank account for her and each week put in 75 percent of his allowance so that when she was older and more likely to be haunted by the abuse she would have funds for therapy.

Restitution is not retribution. It is not vindictiveness. It isn't done to punish the offender or to "get even." It is instead part of an appropriate process of holding the offender accountable for his sin and calling him to repentance and salvation. It is an important act of justice-making. Whether or not the victim feels a personal need for restitution, God's people are called to "do justice" (Micah 6:8) and be advocates for the vulnerable and oppressed. Victimized people find it easier to move on in their process of forgiveness if they have some sense that justice has been done (Fortune, 1983).

## What Forgiveness Isn't

*Forgiveness is not forgetfulness*. Forgiveness based on forgetfulness is "a Christian version of a frontal lobotomy" (Allender, 1990, p. 15). It not only doesn't work to try to forget a piece of personal history as significant as sexual abuse, it isn't desirable. To forget personal history is to deny the very person the survivor has become. It does dishonor to the victim and her story. She cannot understand and rejoice in who she is today if she does not recall the journey which has brought her here. Her experience of God's grace is limited if she forgets important pieces of her life.

Because Christians have been uneasy confronting sexual abuse, the tendency to push for forgetfulness is understandable. If victims would quickly forgive and forget, then we wouldn't have to keep talking about something that makes us so uncomfortable.

If victims forgot the abuse, then they'd stop asking hard questions like: "Where was God when this was happening to me?" "How could someone who was supposed to love me and protect me instead abuse me?" "Why didn't my abuser's professed faith keep him from hurting me?" "Where was the church when this was happening to me?" "With all the emphasis on peace and justice in our denomination, how come none of that concern trickled down to affect the way we lived together as a family?"

David Augsburger has rightly said, "When forgiveness denies that there is anger, acts as if it never happened, smiles as though it never hurts, fakes as though it is all forgotten . . . it is not forgiveness. It's a magical fantasy" (Augsburger, 1981, p. 52).

*Forgiveness is not excusing the abuse.* To forgive my abuser is not to say, "It's okay. I know you didn't mean to hurt me this much." It's not saying, "Well I know you had a hard childhood too and you couldn't really control yourself." Forgiveness is neither making excuses for the wretchedness of the abuse nor minimizing the pain it has caused.

Counselors and pastors often encourage victims to humanize and understand their offender by focusing on his pain and possible victimization as a child. This may be helpful in the process of forgiveness, but it must never be presented in a way which manipulates the victim into excusing or condoning the abuse. Yes, we all have feet of clay. Yes, we all do things of which we are ashamed. But awareness of this does not mean sexual abuse is excusable. It may be forgivable; it is never excusable.

One victim says, "I had been taught that blame was unchristian. So I kept trying to excuse my abusive grandfather, kept saying he didn't really want to hurt me, didn't really know what he was doing. But I found I couldn't truly forgive him until I understood how deeply he had wronged me."

*Forgiveness is not absolving the offender.* The victim of abuse does not forgive the offender so his heart is made pure, his record made clean. This is neither her responsibility nor in her power. Absolution for sin is something only God can extend.

Nevertheless, one woman was pressured by her family to forgive an abusive uncle "so he can go to heaven." Another young girl was begged to forgive her incestuous father "so God can forgive him." To put pressure on a victim to absolve her abuser is not only cruel and insensitive, it is also bad theology.

*Forgiveness is not spiritualizing the abuse.* Extending forgiveness to another is a profoundly spiritual act and may result in spiritual growth. But it is not a way of avoiding the pain. It is not something done quickly or flippantly to avoid the terror of woundedness.

Spiritualization of the abuse may be indicated in these comments: "I know God wants me to forgive my abuser and concentrate on the good things that have come out of this, so please stop making me remember and talk about what he did to me. That's all in my past and I just want to move on."

Or, "It's not important to talk about what effect my abuse has had on me because I forgave him a long time ago. I've turned it all over to Jesus. I just want to understand how I ended up with three divorces."

Most victims of childhood sexual abuse survive by denying their true feelings, blaming themselves for what happened, and pretending things really weren't so bad. As adults some tend to follow this same coping pattern, "adding a sugarcoated spirituality to the recipe" (Feldmeth and Finley, 1990, p. 129). While this provides a temporary way of dealing with the emotional pain, it is not forgiveness.

***Forgiveness is not becoming a doormat.*** Christians have been taught to turn the other cheek, to love those who misuse us, and to forgive seventy times seven times. However, Christian forgiveness is not to say passively, "It's okay. I'm not worth very much anyway. Whatever you do, I'll forgive you." Forgiveness is not passive resignation to man's tendency to dominate and overpower others. Neither is it giving in to woman's tendency to give up too much for too little in return.

***Forgiveness doesn't mean the abuser is trusted.*** Forgiveness and trust are two different processes. If a victim of abuse chooses to forgive her abuser, it does not necessarily mean she can or should trust him to be alone with vulnerable children. Pastors and others have mistakenly told victims that if they don't trust their abuser they haven't really forgiven him.

Treatment for sexual offenses is difficult, long term and sometimes ineffective. Unless a perpetrator has been through such treatment and has a mechanism for continual support and accountability, he is no safer alone with children than is an untreated alcoholic alone with a corkscrew in a wine cellar.

Many perpetrators are frustrated that they have apologized for having abused their adult daughters as children, have been forgiven by the victim, yet are not allowed to spend time alone with their grandchildren. An additional misfortune is that the nonoffending grandparent's access to the grandchildren is likewise curtailed. This is one more tragic, inevitable consequence of abuse. But in families with a history of sexual abuse, vulnerable children's well-being and safety must be put ahead of adults' desires.

## What Forgiveness Is

Forgiveness is an important relational theme in the Bible. *Salah* is the primary Hebrew word we translate as "to forgive." It occurs forty-six times in the Old Testament and refers to God removing sin from the people. Two other words also refer to forgiveness—*kapar* (to cover or atone for wrongdoing) and *nasa* (to lift up a sin and carry it away).

In the New Testament, the primary Greek word we translate as "to forgive" is *aphiemi*. It occurs twenty-two times (Vine, 1985). Aphiemi has the connotation of sins sent away, divine punishment remitted, and harmony between God and the sinner restored. Aphiemi is accomplished through repentance and acceptance of Christ's death and resurrection, which makes new life possible (Enright, Eastin, Golden, Sarinopoulos, and Freedman, 1992).

Religious people of all times and persuasions have understood the power of forgiveness and have endeavored to teach and practice it. Currently, even nonreligious self-help circles are emphasizing the power of forgiveness for inner healing of past hurts. Forgiveness is a way to heal the self and a damaged relationship. It is a way of restoring community. Those who work with victims of sexual abuse usually agree that some form of forgiveness is crucial to recovery from childhood victimization.

While forgiveness is primarily an act of the will, a conscious decision, it cannot come just because an authority orders it. Forgiveness is not a simple statement of "that's okay." Forgiveness is a process which allows the victim to let go of the intense emotional pain associated with her abuse and replace it with inner resolution and peace. Forgiveness disarms the power of abuse to continue causing pain and turmoil and revictimization. Forgiveness says,

> I will no longer allow this experience to dominate my life. I will not let it continue to make me feel bad about myself. I will not let it limit my ability to love and trust others in my life. I will not let my memory of the experience continue to victimize and control me (Fortune, 1983, p. 209).

An important step in the forgiveness process is for a victim to forgive herself for the things she may have done which were perhaps painful and destructive but were a means of coping with the abuse. Gentleness toward self may be hard but is important in letting go of inappropriate self-blame for the abuse.

Because children are developmentally egocentric, everything that happens to them gets interpreted through egocentric eyes. Thus the natural childish tendency is to internalize blame. "It must have happened to me because I was a bad girl . . . was provocative . . . upset my mother so she couldn't give him what he needed . . . somehow wanted it . . . didn't have the courage to stop it or run away."

Self-blame and unconscious guilt lead to self-destructive behaviors in adult victims. Self-blame may cause victims unconsciously to cling to problems and pain to keep punishing themselves. Forgiveness thus begins with forgiving the childhood self and perhaps a child's body for responding to abuse. Forgiveness may involve forgiving the adult body for ongoing self-abusive behaviors and the adult heart for taking so long to heal.

When the victim has given up self-blame and personal guilt for the abuse, she may be ready to feel the full depth of her anger, her hurt, her terror. This realistic appraisal of the victim's own emotional pain and of the offender's considerable injustice are a critical step in the forgiveness process (Enright, Eastin, Golden, Sarinopoulos, and Freedman, 1992).

Rage, indignation, and despair are likely to result as the victims moves into this stage. It is critical that she be surrounded by loving, strong people who can offer her the support and protection she needs at this vulnerable time. It takes much time and energy to feel and evaluate the full extent of the damage caused by abuse. This is a difficult time for the victim and those around her. No wonder there is a tendency to rush her through this stage.

Truth-telling is an important part of this process. The victim must be able to tell someone about the abuse and the pain. If her abuse was pastoral, representatives of the church will need to listen to all the painful, uncomfortable facts. The deeper the pain, the more often the victim will need to tell her story.

Elisabeth Gingrich wrote this poem about the process of healing and forgiveness as she has experienced it in her life.

**A Spiraling Process**

> From darkness and depression
> to circles and cycles and
> ebbs and flows
> of relief and etchings of light
> back into darkness and fears and struggles long into the night.
> Yet followed by something called grace—which turned
> into something that resembled "resurrection"
> the tombstone  s l o w l y  was pushed aside
> and something within me let go and cried. . . .
> But who am I now in the light?
> The story rolled out
> and the story's been told
> and now more healing waits to unfold
> and do you know . . . for the first time in my life I'm stumped,
> at least in this way,
> by the word *forgiveness.*
> What does it mean?
> And just how do I extend it—when I've been so deeply hurt?
> O teach me, Mother God, about *forgiveness*
> in a spiraling kind of way,
> for it strikes me as awesome and deep
> and I need time for it
> to sit and steep
> into my heart
> and body
> and soul.

Rarely does the process of forgiveness move in an efficient, tidy, linear way. More often forgiveness moves in a spiraling kind of way from the Spirit's gentle first nudgings, to determined attempts to release the anger, then back to struggles with pain, then more strength and commitment to let go of the captivating power of despair. With time and healing, the central painful core exerts less controlling power. With each circuit, the victims finds herself at a higher, freer level than the last.

If the victim experiences some measure of justice and restitution, she will find it easier to forgive her abuser. In instances of pastoral abuse, official acknowledgment from her church, expression of deep sorrow that she has been violated, and assurance that steps are being taken to protect other victims from the offender's behavior may be enough. Perhaps she will ask for costs of counseling which have resulted from her victimization. She should be asked what she needs so she can feel some token of justice has been done.

After the victim has placed blame where it properly belongs, has felt the depth of her pain and woundedness, and has experienced some measure of justice and restitution, she is more likely to integrate the abuse experience into her life. She may then see the abuse as one part of her life story instead of the only part. The abuse will always be there if she chooses to pull it out, look at the experience again, and feel the feelings.

But now she can make a choice. The abuse isn't an uncontrollable wave of terror ready to overwhelm her at any moment. Integrating the abuse into the overall journey of her life is an important step in the forgiveness process and a way of freeing her from her painful past. One survivor of abuse recalls, "I knew I was starting to forgive my father when I was able to see myself as more than a victim of sexual abuse, and my father as more than a sex offender."

Listen to what other survivors of sexual abuse say when talking about the process of forgiveness in their lives. "I think I've started to forgive my grandfather because this fall I was thinking of him and missing the fun times we used to have picking apples together in his orchard."

One woman shares, "I had been working real hard at forgiving my father. When I next saw him, he looked much smaller than I'd ever remembered him. Before I'd experienced him as very big and muscular and terrifying. I felt a wave of compassion for the sad-looking little man he now was."

Another victim says, "I realized I had started forgiving my father when I became aware there was a part of me capable of doing the same thing to someone else that he had done to me. That realization humanized him for me and showed me I was starting to forgive."

Yet another shares, "I knew I was moving toward forgiveness when I was genuinely able to hope that good things happened to my abuser and to sincerely wish him well."

## Reconciliation

Reconciliation is the ideal we work toward when forgiveness has been extended. It is possible only when the offender's destructive behaviors and intentions have changed. When there is true repentance and forgiveness, then reconciliation may occur.

Estranged people torn apart because of abuse may experience a healthy, wholesome relationship for the first time in their lives. When a person holds out a hand in forgiveness to the one who has wronged, she is saying, "Come on back to me, I want to be your friend."

In the case of family sexual abuse, she may be saying, "Come back into my life, I want to be your daughter" (Smedes, 1984, p. 32). Smedes further notes that the price of the ticket for walking together again is for the one who has committed the wrong to be truthful and honest about the reality of the estranged relationship, about the victim's pain, and the offender's responsibility for that pain.

Congregations must work with victims and offenders to bring them to the place where reconciliation is possible. This is important kingdom business. It is also rewarding work. Few experiences are as powerfully moving as the coming together of true repentance and forgiveness in reconciliation. The angels in heaven must surely do cartwheels of ecstatic joy when two people who have been estranged and isolated in their pain embrace in love, reconciliation, and renewed relationship.

What does a victim do when her abuser denies he ever did anything wrong to her, calls her a liar, accuses her of fantasizing? In these situations, reconciliation cannot happen. The relationship can not be restored. At best, the two may establish a superficial peaceful coexistence dependent on the continuing denial of truth.

Many a victim who has confronted her abuser in an attempt to crumble the alienating wall of denial lives with the frustration of not being able to bring about restored relationship. She may continue to seek this ideal reconciliation and be repeatedly defeated, thus locking herself in agonizing frustration.

Another option when the abuser continues to deny the abuse is for the victim to choose to extend a kind of unilateral forgiveness. While *reconciliation* requires both that the offender confess and change his behavior and that the offended extend forgiveness, it is possible unilaterally to let go of the anger and pain caused by abuse. It is possible to let go of the pain and anger caused by another's offense even when the requirements for reconciliation have not been met, even when the offender has not asked for forgiveness.

By letting go, the offended refuses to let herself be held captive by the offender's unwillingness to repent. In letting go, the abuse is robbed of its power to be an ongoing source of pain, despair, and frustration. Extending unrequested forgiveness empowers the survivor. It frees her to experience God's grace, healing, and joy in her life despite lack of reconciliation with her offender. Surely the heavenly hosts rejoice when a survivor takes this difficult and courageous step.

## Chapter 8

# Congregational Responses to Abuse

It is understandably disturbing to learn how common sexual abuse is in Christian homes and churches. Some people feel depressed, hopeless, and immobilized as they face the magnitude and implications of the problem. Nevertheless, individuals and congregations must channel their distress and concern about abuse into developing effective ways of comforting and protecting victims, bringing abusers into a right relationship with God or their victims, and working to prevent further violation of vulnerable people.

This will not be an easy; the task is not for the faint of heart. It will require commitment to bring light, truth, and justice to a painful reality which we have preferred to ignore and deny. It will require rethinking basic assumptions we hold about men, women, and children; about the Creation and the Fall; and about our physical bodies and their relationship to spirituality.

## Congregational Support for Victims of Sexual Abuse

How can congregations become havens of safety and compassionate resource centers for people brutalized by sexual abuse? How can congregations extend healing love and support to victims?

Perhaps the most important step a congregation can take is to make a conscious decision to dislodge the wall of secrecy and denial which has surrounded sexual abuse among Christians. The silence surrounding sexual abuse must be broken before either the victim, the offender, their families, or their congregations can be healed.

By acknowledging the problem and publicly naming the sin of abuse, victims come to understand that their stories are similar to stories of many Christian families. Their private shame may decrease as they begin to understand they are not alone.

How can victims be expected to share their stories of abuse with people who haven't even acknowledged the existence of such a problem among them? When sexual abuse is named in the church, victims may come to see the church as a likely and appropriate place to go for support in their painful journeys toward healing.

In spite of good intentions, a male pastor is usually not an appropriate person to do therapy with female survivors of abuse. Beyond the lack of specialized training to deal with abuse issues, there are factors related to the pastor's maleness which may be stumbling blocks for the survivor. Some congregations are choosing teams of laypeople to get special training in the area of sexual abuse. These teams are trained to stand in loving solidarity with victims who identify themselves within the congregation. They stay informed about additional resources available within the community which may supplement congregational support for victims.

Other congregations have information-sharing sessions for anyone interested in learning how to be supportive friends and listeners to victims. Professional training is not needed to develop basic skills for being lovingly present with persons as they face their abusive past. Here are important guidelines for laypeople and pastoral staff working with abuse victims.

**1. *Assure the victim you will stand with her as she goes through the pain of remembering*.** Human beings are too fragile to walk through profound grief alone. If at some point you feel overwhelmed and unable to continue hearing her story, assure her you will put her in contact with someone else. Find someone in the congregation or professional community who will walk with her.

**2. *Don't take on more than you can handle*.** Encourage the victim to work with a professional therapist who specializes in the treatment of sexual abuse. If she cannot afford professional counseling, ask the congregation to subsidize the cost. Assure her you will be her supportive friend even if you unable to be her therapist.

**3. *Validate her feelings*.** They may be overwhelming, but don't try to talk her out of them. Minimizing the depth of her agony is counterproductive and will only tell her you don't understand. This may cause her to believe she is so bad and defiled she can never relate to the congregation or God. Let her be angry. Don't tell her she shouldn't feel the feelings she has.

**4. *Respect her own process of healing and timetable for recovery*.** Remember the process is different for each survivor. Don't try to push her toward forgiveness until she is ready.

**5. *Listen carefully as she attempts to find meaning in her pain and asks hard questions*.** Don't act shocked when she rages at God and expresses crises of faith.

**6. *Be aware of her feelings of powerlessness*.** Support her efforts to take control of her own life. Stand with her as she tries to make her own decisions about what is best for her.

**7. *Hope for her when she can't hope for herself*.** Assure her that healing is possible, that spiritual and professional resources are available, and that you or someone else will stand by her as she faces her abuse and does the painful work of recovery.

**8. *Develop a team of prayer partners*.** Ask the team to pray for the victim and for you, the support person, as together you walk through the pain of her abuse.

**9. *Take care of your own needs*.** Replenish yourself spiritually, emotionally, and physically. It is exhausting work, even for a professional, to be with someone facing her abuse. Know your limits; don't exceed them. Surround yourself with supportive people and spiritual resources.

**10. *Remind yourself that healing is a gift of grace from God*.** You are a helpful friend in the process, but healing does not depend on you alone.

Many survivors of sexual abuse never have the opportunity to speak of their abuse openly in the congregation. Survivor Cathy Gehman did speak at a church meeting, however. This is what she said.

> I sometimes think I would rather be in a wheelchair than have mental and emotional pain. If I had been crippled by a drunk driver, it would be easy for others to understand why I'm still in a wheelchair or why I need to have an operation now and then. People wouldn't say, "That's in the past, you should get over it," because the wheelchair would be plain evidence that even though the deed is past, the wounds are present.
>
> When Jesus healed a crippled woman, the Pharisees got mad at him for healing on the Sabbath. Sometimes I feel people are unaccepting of the method of my healing, or the time it takes. But Jesus said, "Ought not this woman, a daughter of Abraham whom Satan bound for eighteen long years, be set free from this bondage on the sabbath day?" (Luke 13:16)
>
> The people were displeased with Jesus' timing, but Jesus was grieved that this woman had been without help for eighteen long years. Two or three or five years of healing and admitting truth is not nearly as distressing as twenty years of hidden pain and pretending. Truth so long concealed from even me takes long to be revealed.
>
> Some people seem to think that because I'm a Christian I shouldn't be broken or incapacitated by my emotional pain. I can agree with theology about being victorious through Christ's resurrection power. I know Christ is my healer. I know the Holy Spirit is my source of strength and power. I acknowledge my need to continually grow in faith.
>
> But I also believe the truth is what sets me free, and the truth is

that I carried for twenty years a burden that finally broke me physically and emotionally. Denying my pain and trauma and painting plastic smiles didn't free me. In fact, burying my true feelings and pain so deeply and for so long—because they were too overwhelming for the child-me to face—is why they are so complicated and intense now.

Only as I am allowing my true emotions for the first time to come out into the light am I also experiencing feelings of God's love, of joy, of strength I haven't known before. My very feelings—as confused and irrational as they are—are a sign that I am alive and emerging from years of dead emotional numbness.

If I were merely feeling sorry for myself, I wouldn't be paying hundreds of dollars to work through the trauma. I wouldn't be on medication to stabilize the chemical imbalance in my brain. I wouldn't be waking up several nights a week frightened and sometimes not recognizing my husband. I wouldn't be consulting expensive specialists. I wouldn't have gone into the hospital. This process is too costly and too painful to go through out of mere self-pity. Self-pity is weak, not courageous as I am to face what I have. I know the only way out is through the pain.

I've read a lot of literature and talked with a lot of people—Christian and non-Christian—about the kind of trauma I am recovering from. All the sources confirm that healing is a long process, usually involving years of therapy.

Maybe some of you who have your own history of suffering and have recovered in different ways or in shorter amounts of time. But I have to go through my own process and only God knows how long it takes. Believe me, I want more desperately than anyone for this to end.

I believe Christ bore my sorrows even as he bore my sins in his suffering and death. I acknowledge to him the truth of my emotional devastation and pour out my pain to him in the same way that I put my sins on his cross through confession.

Sanctification doesn't come instantly; I have to confess again and again. But gradually I become more like Christ. Healing doesn't come instantly either, and the deeper rooted the pain is, the longer it takes to place it, through prayer, on the cross.

Even though it may be painful to hear, survivors of abuse need opportunities to share their stories in the congregation. It may be important for their healing and for the congregation's understanding of how to minister to other abused people in the church.

The following account was written by a Christian woman who became sexually involved with a church leader. It was written to describe the role her local congregation played in her healing and recovery from the pastoral abuse and her subsequent suicide attempt.

It's been nine months since I first spilled my secret; seven months since I took the overdose. I never intended to air my secret so publicly. But then I never knew how difficult it would be to live with the telling. I had sworn on my life never to tell.

I wish it could have been done otherwise. As trite as this may sound, "I couldn't help it." I just couldn't see my way through. It got so dark! And so, with only twenty-four hours remaining until my appointment with a psychologist who specializes in victims of abuse, I was admitted to a psychiatric ward in a hospital twenty miles from home.

I remember my stay well, which in retrospect seems odd—I felt so absent. Numb. Frozen. I remember the tears, the rivers, no—the torrents of tears. At first a quiet drip, drip, then a steady dribble, then a pouring—and finally a gushing. Endless tears. My face burned; my body froze.

Tears and questions, both mine and others'. That is what I came home to two days later. At first, I didn't want to see anyone. Only my pastor, his wife, and my sister-in-law had received permission to see me in the hospital. That changed when I returned home. Then, seemingly, everyone wanted—no, needed—to visit.

My children greeted me with "Mommy, why didn't you tell us you were sick?"

"It's not your fault," I told them. They hugged me.

"Did we do something? Is it our fault?" my parents asked.

"Maybe you should just scream it out," suggested my mother-in-law.

"We all have our things," one of my sisters told me. The other said, "It doesn't matter what it is, we're here for you."

"You had us pretty worried," said my brother. Greetings and get-well wishes traveled via phone from my two other brothers.

"Something has happened to me, but I can't say it yet," I told the steady stream of friends who phoned or came by just to hug and say "I love you."

Later the ones who cared enough to feel hurt by what I'd done returned with questions and feelings—anger, betrayal, ambivalence. But still with love.

"Feel what you need to feel," I told them. "This event deserves to be met with outrage and disappointment." Their love compensated for—no, far outweighed—the sharp, piercing words they used to describe what they were feeling.

But their love dug far deeper than their words. "I want to understand this. Help me figure this out," said one well-meaning visitor.

The words rankled. I couldn't yet understand what I'd participated in. The *how's*, *why's*, *what's* all still hung unanswered in my own mind. Oh, the endless unanswerable questions. I didn't need anyone to add to my own still growing list. That visit wasn't helpful.

Another person brought advice. "It seems to me that a lot of 'I'm sorrys' need to be said. But you can't keep looking back. Just get on with your life." With her words my earth-shattering experience shrank into a minimal indiscretion. With but a few words she had denied me the right to process, to interpret my past, to reclaim my future. That also wasn't helpful.

Some people, though not many, avoided me. Not, I think, because of indifference but because of their personal discomfort at the nature of my transgression. How could she? How dare she? were questions that barred them from making contact.

For some such people guilt followed. "You poor child," said a woman to me one Sunday after I left a service in tears. "I'm sorry I haven't talked to you. I was so confused."

Such responses helped, but not I think, as the giver intended. I realized then I wasn't poor or a child. And I didn't want pity. This was an adult experience. With the telling I became a survivor, not a poor victim.

My church. My home. How to go back? Would this prodigal daughter still be welcomed and wanted? My congregation rolled out the red carpet. Twelve flower arrangements in a rainbow of colors invited me back. "Please recover. We love you," came the message. Cards trickled in, delivering hope and promises to pray on our behalf. My mother asked if I had any idea how many people were praying for me. "There are hundreds," she said.

I went back. How could I not? At first with fear and trembling, safely tucked in the back pew where I thought no one would see me. Afterward I slunk out to our van, hoping, hoping not to be noticed.

From across the parking lot two women loudly shouted my name. "Hello!"

Sunday after Sunday the same scenario. I was still wanted, still worthy. A touch on the arm, a quick hug, a joining of hands, a smile; even silence couldn't stifle the love my church bestowed on me. I'll never forget the day I walked across the large foyer. A sinner in a marathon, cheered by grace incarnate.

The following Sunday I repeated the trek, this time with unaverted eyes. Several weeks later my family moved several pews forward. On Christmas Eve we sat in the front row. "Silent night, Holy night." I sang along.

What has helped? The love, the patience, the acceptance, and the honesty. The reminders of who I am and continue to be. "Your gifts of love and care have not been exorcised," someone wrote to me. "We read David's laments, so why not yours, too?" wrote one friend. She encouraged me to keep writing.

"We decided to take our cues from you," a couple told us as we drove the hour-long drive home from dinner at a lovely restaurant. More memorable, however, was the visit. I enjoyed it, truly enjoyed it, without effort. True friends gave space but also hope. They recognized that this journey would take time and more time. Hope was the light ahead.

Did words come easily to anyone in those first few months? That is something I do not take for granted. I saw the struggle in people's faces as they chose their words. "I give you my unconditional love. I hope you stay in our small group." Those words came out in a slow stutter.

"I want to love you with the love of God," said another friend. I wondered if she'd ever be able to move past her anger. A week later, she visited me. She told me she was feeling the stirrings of compassion. My doubts about her commitment to our friendship were laid to rest.

Still I'm finding it difficult to trust again. I feel so crippled, especially relationally. But that is my issue, not my friends'. In my wildest dreams I couldn't ever have imagined the outpouring of love with which my friends gifted me.

Over and over the people in my life invited me, called me back to life. They remembered me to myself. And somewhere, somehow, though I do not recall the precise moment, I not only came back to life, I rediscovered who I am. With that I began the search to find my place in life again.

No Bible story reflects my recent homecoming as well as the

story of the prodigal son. "For this son of mine was dead and is alive again; he was lost and is found."

No one brought this passage to such profound aliveness as did my friend Marie. She entered my experience and came alongside in a quiet but powerful and healing way. First she sent a card in which she expressed her love for me and said nothing is beyond redemption. If I would let God in, God would transform this experience into something good.

Marie offered to be a companion but would wait for me to initiate contact. With that, she gave me an invaluable gift: she gave me a sense of control. In my seemingly most powerless state, someone gave me a choice. How could I not respond affirmatively?

I took my time and she waited. We made a date. With shame and nervousness, I approached her apartment door. I knocked. My hand had not yet fallen to my side when there she stood. Arms spread wide open and then suddenly, wrapped around me.

"I love you," she said.

Then she ushered me to a chair which faced a large picture of Jesus, in a pose similar to the one she'd greeted me with. Arms wide open, hands beckoning to draw nearer. A caption would have been redundant; the eyes said it all. God had not turned his back on me. "For this my daughter was dead and is alive again, was lost and is found."

I am, I suspect, one of the fortunate ones. My family has stood by me, as have my friends and our church. I have a husband who loves me enough to be angry at what happened, but who also loves me too much to turn his back, or worse, use this experience to control me. He set the tone for our future together when he brought me home from the hospital. "This is our home," he said, "and our life."

Love. That is what has helped the most. God-love, shown through people-love. Home. How could I not return? I am grateful beyond measure for the love and support I've had on my journey.

## Congregational Role with Offenders

A congregation which becomes aware that a member is a sexual abuser is forced either to pretend it doesn't know (thus making it possible for business to continue as usual) or to struggle with disturbing, painful, awkward issues. Beyond the initial shock following the disclosure of offense, the congregation is

forced to face the reality of evil—not just in the world but among
its own brothers and sisters.

Sometimes people who call themselves Christians, people
who sit with us in church Sunday after Sunday, *do* allow evil into
their lives. The very people with whom we take communion and
who teach our Sunday school classes or preach our sermons
sometimes *do* choose evil over goodness, *do* choose death-
inducing instead of life-giving behaviors.

Sexual violation forces us to face the wretchedness of sin—sin
in our very own community of faith. As congregational members listen to the pain of victims, often violated by Christians
they trusted and loved, they may find themselves overcome
with despair about the depravity of the human condition. A congregation may experience a kind of corporate depression, a loss
of energy, of hope, of joy. This may particularly be the case if the
offender was a leader in the congregation or denomination.

Congregations will be forced to grapple with important theological questions: Do we acknowledge the possibilities of new
life in Christ? Do we believe God can heal both wounded bodies
and ravished souls? Do we believe broken relationships can be
restored? Do we have the right to confront personal sin in others
or is that God's job? While we believe in turning the other cheek,
can we confront evil? Do we believe God is greater than evil? Do
we truly believe God's grace and forgiveness can cover even sins
we find repugnant and reprehensible?

To work effectively and redemptively with offenders in the
congregation, the church must reaffirm its belief in the power of
the resurrection and the possibility of new life in Christ for both
offender and offended. Although steps that must be taken toward new life will be difficult, the congregation must hold out a
vision of new life for the victim, the victimizer, and families of
both.

While passionately clinging to the hope of resurrection and
new life, congregations must cautiously determine the most appropriate and helpful steps toward that goal. To do this they
must be aware of certain common tendencies among sex offenders.

Many working in the field have observed that denial is great among offenders. As Judith Herman (1981, p. 22) says, "Denial has always been the incestuous father's first line of defense." Many sexual offenders outright deny the abuse. Others minimize the full extent of their abusive behavior and acknowledge only a small part of their actions. "Yes, I did fondle her breasts a few times but I certainly wouldn't ever have gone further."

Other offenders admit their behavior but justify it. "It really didn't hurt her." "It was good for her." "How was I supposed to resist her when she wore that provocative little gown?" "She was curious and I was just teaching her a few things she'll need to know in a few years anyway."

Some offenders admit to the behaviors but deny responsibility. Sometimes they blame their drinking, stress at work, their wives' lack of interest in sex, their own "over-developed sex drive." These behaviors allow offenders to externalize the problem and keep them from taking responsibility for the abuse.

Most laypeople in a congregation are not prepared for the extent nor tenacity of denial in sex offenders. Consequently, they may easily be convinced that an offender is telling the truth when in fact he is denying the extent of his sin and his responsibility for the pain he has caused another. Being swayed by an offender's eloquent denial may keep him from facing the darkness of his heart and make it less likely he will experience repentance, redemption, and restoration.

Congregations likewise need to be aware that "religious conversions" are common among convicted offenders. They often show extreme remorse when caught and convicted. After their "conversions" they are inclined to insist they don't need treatment now but will instead pray more, read the Bible more, and be more active in church activities. They promise to rely more on God. They may manipulate church members or the pastor into testifying for them as character witnesses in an attempt to avoid the full legal penalty of their offense.

Of course, true conversion may occur among sex offenders and is to be desired. How then can true conversions be distinguished from religious conversions whose primary goal is the evasion of treatment for sexual abuse? Salter (1988) observes that the difference lies in whether or not the person sees his new experience with God as empowering him to change his behavior through treatment—or eliminating the need for treatment. Congregations must understand that offenders will abuse again unless they admit their problems and receive specialized treatment. Even admitting abusiveness and getting therapy may not guarantee that the offender will not abuse again but these are important steps toward preventing further abuse.

The perpetrator of sexual abuse who has been caught is forced to wrestle with his personal shame and sin before God and his accusers. Suicidal threats and gestures are not uncommon as the offender is forced to face his personal depravity, shame, and destructiveness. This may be a pivotal point in the offender's journey. He may erect higher barriers of denial around his soul. Or he may fall on his knees in true repentance before God and his fellow believers and begin his journey toward healing.

The pastor or congregational people who are close to him play a vital role at this point in his journey. They must assure him that even though they are grieved and angry about his sin against another, they love him and are committed to walking with him through his difficult next steps. They must be confrontive to ensure he gets the treatment that will prevent his abusing again. If he has been convicted by the courts, the congregation should make sure he cooperates with the legal system. If he hasn't been legally charged, the congregation should use its authority and influence to see that the offender is treated for sexual abuse.

Congregations need to understand the importance of getting professional help for sexual offenders. Sexual abuse requires specialized treatment. It is not something laypeople, no matter how wise or well intentioned, can provided for the offender. Without specialized treatment, the offender is likely to abuse again.

Unfortunately, even after professional treatment the abuser may abuse again. Through therapy the offender can learn ways to be honest about his propensity for abuse and ways to make sure he isn't in situations where he may be likely to return to abuse.

Recovery from the sin of abuse is a daily, ongoing process. Most professionals who work with sex offenders believe perpetrators need maintenance counseling for the rest of their lives. Congregations can provide the kind of accountability needed to ensure that offenders get and stay with the help they need never to abuse again. Congregations can firmly and lovingly say, "Because we love you, we won't tolerate abusive behavior anymore. We're going to name this sin and make sure you get the help you need to never abuse again." A Twelve Step program can be an important component of recovery and accountability for offenders and may be one in which congregations ask offender to engage.

Congregations may also need to say to past abusers, "Because we love our children and because we love you, we will not allow you to be in situations where you may be tempted and susceptible to abuse." Because as Christians we place a high priority on forgiveness, it will be difficult but important not to allow past perpetrators of sexual abuse, even if they have repented and sought treatment, to be in positions within the congregation where they have access to and authority over vulnerable children.

The congregation can be instrumental in helping the offender come to true repentance. The biblical term for repentance is *metanoia*. This implies turning from sinful, violent behavior to loving, humane ways of interacting with others.

The congregation must help the offender understand that repentance is much more than saying, "I'm sorry." It is (as discussed in chapter 7) acknowledging the destruction caused another child of God, feeling and confessing the awfulness of the violence committed against her, attempting to make amends and offer restitution, becoming aware of personal weaknesses, and doing everything possible to ensure that the destructive behaviors never again happen.

The congregation can help the perpetrator understand and be accountable as he walks through these steps toward redemption and healing. Even if the overt abuse ended decades ago, there are patterns of thinking which originally led to the abuse and must be confronted, changed, and healed in the perpetrator.

Even if he hasn't abused for years, the untreated perpetrator will need help facing his sin and walking through the steps of repentance, restitution, and forgiveness. He needs to continue working at understanding his ongoing susceptibility to destructive attitudes and behaviors toward women and children.

## Walking with the Family Affected by Abuse

When a family member is publicly accused of sexual abuse, pain and disequilibrium result for the entire family and church community. The following is a true account of one congregation's response to a case of incest in their church family. This account was written by a member of the congregation's pastoral care committee. The story is real but the names are not.

Jack Miller was arrested for molesting his youngest daughter, Mandy. Mandy was his only victim. The Millers were well-known and highly visible in the church. In fact, Jack had been teaching the youth Sunday school class but had just ended his term.

The congregation is small and warm. It is known for its friendliness and support to members in times of crisis. There had already been many opportunities in the congregation to deal with difficulties in an honest, open way. Still there was no precedent for dealing with a tragedy of this magnitude that touched people in such deep and varied ways. It became clear fairly soon that the congregation would be involved in a lengthy, unpredictable process.

The pastoral care committee, a six-member team composed of three pastors employed part-time by the congregation, and three laypeople, shepherded the process. Particularly in the first six months, it felt like walking on a dimly lit path. There was just enough light to determine the next step. Leaders had to trust that future direction would become gradually clear. This, of course, made it impossible to do long-range planning.

The pastoral care committee did determine that there were several subgroups in the congregation and worked at ministering to their unique needs during this time of upheaval. The subgroups included the family—the non-offending spouse, the offender, the victim, and other children in the family; the members of the youth Sunday school class; and other members of the congregation who had little understanding of sexual abuse.

Particular concern was focused on Mandy, the victim. A couple of meetings were held with the family members in the first two weeks after the arrest. The meetings with Jack were separate from the ones with the other family members.

Separate support groups were formed around Jack and Cathy, his wife. The groups were composed of four or five caring congregational members and a member of the pastoral care committee. Each group's purpose was to listen to the individuals, assist them in making decisions, and encourage Jack to take the necessary steps for repentance and healing.

These groups met regularly for a year after the arrest. On several occasions one representative from each group met with Jack and Cathy jointly to help mediate issues where they were stuck. For example, several discussions focused on whether or not their marital relationship could be reconciled.

The entire congregation was informed of the arrest and the charges on the first Sunday after the arrest. A congregational meeting was held on the second Sunday. At that time, members were given the opportunity to speak about their reactions to the offense and the arrest. They were invited to give the pastoral care committee advice on how to proceed.

Most of the talking was done in small discussion groups with a pre-selected leaders/listeners. Whenever the victim, Mandy; wife, Cathy; or other family members were present at these congregational meetings, a supportive group was first formed around them before other groups formed and began talking.

A separate meeting was held for the congregation's young people who had been in Jack's Sunday school class and who were friends of the children of the family. The purpose of this meeting was to give the young people a chance to vent their feelings and support their hurting friends.

Contact was also made with the criminal justice system. A letter was composed on behalf of the congregation and given to the judge and the prosecuting attorney. Jack had confessed his guilt at the time of his arrest and continued to take full responsibility for his actions. The congregational letter outlined the steps the congregation was taking to support this family, to call the offender to accountability, and to educate the congregation in matters of sexual abuse.

Six to ten members of the congregation accompanied Jack and Cathy to court, first when he tabled his appeal and later at the time of his sentencing. The judge solicited advice from congregational representatives at the time of sentencing; he included that advice in his sentencing remarks.

Jack served his sentence on weekends. Congregational members gave him rides to and from jail. In addition to his jail term, Jack was ordered to do community service. Congregational representatives were given responsibility to plan and supervise this service and to report back to officials.

Cathy, Jack, Mandy, and the other children used local counseling services. At times the church paid for this counseling. Financial support was offered at a number of other points, for example to assist Jack in setting up a separate residence. Jack and Cathy also sought financial counseling from a bank at the congregation's encouragement.

The pastoral care committee scheduled a year-long series of related congregational meetings. These included hearing about offenders, listening to a different offender and his family recount their experience, and hearing two other adult survivors of incest tell their story. Some meetings included discussion about the current church family and how to help or proceed. Sometimes the Millers were present; sometimes they deliberately stayed away due to the sensitive nature of the discussion.

The pastoral care committee also made direct and regular contact with other survivors in the congregation—survivors who had been abused by other offenders. Over the months, survivors and their spouses were offered support—counseling, group help, meetings, phone calls, and visits. Some survivors accepted the congregation's offer of financial support so they could receive counseling for the painful issues Jack's presence among them had raised.

Regular memos were written detailing steps being taken and planned. The committee also gave updates regarding Jack, Cathy, and their family and welcomed input as they worked with the Miller family and the broader congregation. These memos were placed in each family's mailbox.

Sexuality education classes were held for the young people. Occasionally young people would attend other congregational meetings. When they did they formed their own small group for discussion.

Jack did not attend church for more than a year. Initially he was forbidden by his bail release order to be in the same place as his children. After that order was withdrawn, the pastoral care committee requested that he stay absent until a number of steps had been taken—that he offer a communication to the congregation about his actions, that his family indicate their willingness for him to be present in church, and that other survivors have time to sort out their responses to his presence.

Jack wrote a letter to the congregation which was read during a Sunday morning worship service seven months after his arrest. Two weeks later the pastoral care committee set up an informal meeting with Jack and whoever wished to come from the congregation. About twenty people came to speak with him.

Sixteen months after his arrest, the pastoral care committee arranged for Jack to attend a social event and a church service. The congregation was given advance notice. More discussion was held between the pastoral care committee and his family, other survivors and their spouses, and congregational members. Eighteen months after his arrest, with the pastoral care committee's supervision, Jack began attending church on a bimonthly basis.

The marital separation, necessitated originally by the arrest, continues. The couple does have regular contact. The children choose what level of interaction they want with their father.

A pastoral care committee member makes these observations.

1. Our congregation could work in this direct and proactive manner because the Millers were willing to be open. Leadership people felt it was important to give accurate information, with sensitivity to prevent damaging rumors. At times the Millers have questioned whether it was good for them to be so public with their problem, fearing "it has gotten out of our hands." Still, they acknowledge it has enabled the congregation to give them a great deal of support and has allowed the congregation to work more openly and effectively.

2. Jack's willingness to take full responsibility for his offenses meant the congregation was spared determining his guilt.

3. This process required enormous output from leaders. The committee felt it was important to follow the direct and heavy course they had set for themselves and the congregation because it had the potential for so much healing.

4. It has been difficult for the congregation. There has been tension and discomfort expressed with the situation and process. Those without direct experience are impatient with the slow process and are pushing for speedy forgiveness and reconciliation. Those who have been sexually abused (and their partners) experience great discomfort at having the topic of sexual abuse "live" in their congregations and having an identified offender sitting in the worship service.

The leadership team subsequently asked a congregational group to plan and implement responses that would assist the healing of other survivors. This group was asked to assist the congregation in providing tangible support to survivors and to help the congregation find ways to lament the sin of sexual abuse.

Outside professionals were used at several points in the congregational processing. It might have been more helpful to have used professionals more frequently.

5. The criminal justice system clearly welcomed the congregation's role in Jack's conviction, sentencing, and rehabilitation.

6. It seems important that churches deal directly with sexual abuse and other forms of violence toward children and family members. It's not going to go away, so it makes sense to deal with it openly, directly, and in ways which offer the best chance of opening the door to repentance, accountability, changed behaviors, healing, forgiveness, and reconciliation.

## Chapter 9
# Making Worship Sensitive to Survivors

Each time the congregation gathers, both victims and perpetrators of abuse are present. Those who plan and lead worship need to keep this sobering but inescapable reality in mind.

Reflect back on the most recent worship service you attended. Imagine you are a victim of sexual abuse. Then imagine you are a perpetrator. What would the service have been like for you? What would the service have communicated to you about the church's willingness to acknowledge your hidden pain? How would the service have touched the secret terror of your heart?

Rituals, liturgies, and prayers often touch the spirit in ways that ordinary words cannot. They can be a powerful tool for reaching in healing ways to the inner depths of someone wounded by abuse. Instead, our public worship may further violate the victim and cause her to feel that no one understands her pain. Congregations should incorporate into their worship litanies, rituals, laments and prayers which name the sin of abuse and which acknowledge the despair of her abused body and soul.

Some rituals of healing may be general enough in language and symbolism that they will touch meaningfully a broad spectrum of victims and will be appropriate for public worship services. Some survivors have chosen to work with a therapist, friends, or a small support group to create a uniquely personal ritual to celebrate the journey from brokenness to healing. A ritual designed for the particular story and needs of the individual survivor can be an important stepping stone toward wholeness.

For a victim whose abuse had a ritualistic component, a ritual of healing may be particularly significant. Symbols such as candles, boxes, or certain garments which may have been used in her ritualistic abuse may be included in the healing ceremony to reclaim the power of those objects for good.

My friend Joyce writes, "Sometimes I fantasize about real ceremonies of healing and blessing. What would they consist of? Chanting, incantations, rituals. I imagine movement for the forgiveness and beseeching sections; bells, clapping, and light for the justice parts. And of course, some oil. Wouldn't it be wonderful?"

Joyce further notes that survivors need to be able to express with their whole bodies, in the context of the believing church, the shame and deep anguish which they feel. "Survivors should not have to leave their shame outside the church door but should be invited to bring it into the congregational setting for healing and blessing."

Because the violence was experienced in the survivor's body, healing will need to acknowledge and restore her traumatized body as well as her wounded soul. Congregations should work with survivors interested in developing personal rituals for healing.

Lay therapist and church elder Cathryn Passmore notes the importance of including the survivor in the planning of healing rituals. She sees her primary role as that of a caring listener who encourages people to discover what feels personally safe, authentic, and meaningful for them.

One healing ritual in which she participated took place along a riverbank. The abused woman burned a photo of her abuser to symbolize "burning the bridge" of inappropriate sexual contact and power over her. She then spontaneously scooped up river water, symbolic for her of Christ's limitless compassion and healing power, and washed away all ashes from the burned photograph.

Cathryn believes it is crucial to be sensitive to spontaneous movements of the Spirit in healing rituals. "I find it is often the unplanned components which allow for the most significant bursts of God's healing touch."

I have conducted rituals of confession and mourning for perpetrators. One man brought a photo of himself and his daughter to a therapy session. This photo had been taken shortly before he began abusing her. He made from construction paper a black envelope which symbolized for him the darkness and evil which had characterized his relationship with her from the time the abuse began.

After placing his daughter's photograph inside the black envelope, he held it near his heart, rocked slowly back and forth, and cried loud and deep for the lost years and relationship with his daughter and for the profound pain he had caused her. Later he removed the photograph, tore the black envelope into little pieces, and wrote a letter to his now-adult daughter, asking what she needed him to do before they began rebuilding a relationship.

Some months later I helped this man write a litany of mourning and confession. He invited several close friends from his congregation to participate with him in a service of lamentation where he shared his story, confessed his sin, and read his litany. Then his friends surrounded him, laid hands on him, and prayed for his forgiveness and healing. These rituals, one performed in the privacy of a therapist's office and the other shared publicly with Christian friends, seemed to be pivotal stepping stones in the healing journey of this perpetrator.

One congregation had a ceremony of "binding" and "loosening" (see Matt. 16:19) for an incest perpetrator who had been an active member. This followed several years of intense congregational involvement with the perpetrator and his family as he cooperated with the judiciary system, got counseling, confronted his evil, confessed his sin, and worked toward forgiveness and reconciliation with his family.

In the ceremony he was bound (forbidden) from involvement in church assignments and activities which would put him in contact with vulnerable children and young people. However, he was loosened (given permission) to participate in church activities where he would not have contact with or access to vulnerable people.

Effective rituals may be planned for individuals or groups. After leading a meditation based on John 12 (here Mary of Bethany anoints Jesus with expensive perfume), pastor Mary Berkshire Stueben led a group of women through a healing ritual. It was noted that throughout this story Mary never speaks. Judas attacks and Jesus defends—but Mary is silent.

This is something other than women's silence at other places in the biblical narrative and throughout much of history. Mary doesn't speak. But she acts. She doesn't ask permission and she doesn't try to justify. Mary Berkshire Stueben says, "To act in such an extravagant and decisive manner indicates she is acting from her own sense of authority, an authority she came to realize and own as a student of Jesus."

The ritual was intended to give back to abused women an inner sense of authority. After the meditation, women stood in groups of four or five. Each group had a small bowl of scented oil. First women were invited to anoint themselves—to acknowledge the reality of their own pain and abuse, to trace tears on their own cheeks with a fingertip dipped in oil.

Next each woman was invited to anoint the woman standing beside her. This time the anointing was in the shape of a heart on her forehead, "that our heart might be whole, that our heart and mind together might be healed, and that we might know our own authority and claim our peace!"

Many women write personal prayers and laments as part of their healing journey. They may be willing, if asked, to share these for public worship. Others may be willing to work with a worship planning committee to prepare materials for worship.

The following resources are sensitive to the experience of abused people. They were written for this book and are included as examples of victim-sensitive resources. Feel free to use these or let them inspire you as you create your own.

# Psalm of Blessing

*By Joyce Munro*

You can trust your journey through darkest night,
    for you have light!

God's tenderness surrounds you
    and you are not alone.
You are making your way to the waters of peace,
    and you can ask for help along the journey.

Even though you walk through the valley of deep pain,
    you need not be afraid.
Anger salves the raw wound, and
    tears must flow to cleanse.

In the presence of your enemies,
May healers anoint you with oil,
    Friends spread a table before you,
    and offer you rest;

May God bathe you in stillness,
    breathe with you,
    murmuring comfort
    in the hour when you have lost hope or strength.

For goodness and mercy belong to you
    this day and all the days of your life.
So dance joy,
    laugh loud hallelujahs,
        or leap hosannas.
You deserve God's peace
    And shall dwell in it forever!

## Responsive Reading

*By Elisabeth J. Gingrich*

All:       Oh, God, stay near and bless me with your love.

Reader:   Some days I feel your presence enfolding me with love, but then there are days when I ask, "When will the pain finally go away?"

All:       Oh, God, stay near and bless me with your love.

Reader:   You have taught me about grace and love and of your faithfulness in spite of whatever I face from day to day.

All:       Oh, God, stay near and bless me with your love.

Reader:   God, keep me open to your constant healing process. Keep me open to learning and to letting go of my anger, my pain, and my hurt.
Keep me believing and trusting that my healing and wholeness are being held in the palm of your hand.

All:       Oh, God, stay near and bless me with your tender love, with your gentle embraces, and with your perpetual presence.

# A Responsive Reading for Communion

*Based on Mark 14:22 and 24*
*By Cindy Hines Kurfman*

Leader: While they were eating, Jesus took a loaf of bread, and after blessing it he broke it, gave it to them, and said, "Take, this is my body."

All: As we eat this bread made of flour, we reflect that both this bread and some among us have been pounded by human hands.

Leader: The flour is mixed with salt.

All: We reflect that salt is painful to wounds. We pray that we would not reinjure our sisters and brothers by our words or actions.

Leader: The salt and flour are mixed with oil.

All: We reflect that oil is also used for healing and blessing. We pray for the healing of our sisters and brothers. We ask for God's blessing upon them.

Leader: God, we ask you to bless this broken bread and the broken bodies and spirits of our sisters and brothers. We ask that as we eat this bread you would continue the process of healing.
(Pause for silent prayer and the eating of the bread.)

Leader: Then Jesus took a cup, and after giving thanks he gave it to them and all of them drank from it. He said to them, "This is my blood of the covenant which is poured out for many."

All: As we drink this grape juice, we reflect that both the juice and some among us have been crushed by human hands.

Leader: Wine can be used to cleanse wounds.

All: We ask God to cleanse us spiritually, emotionally, and physically.

Leader: God, we ask you to bless this crushed juice and the crushed bodies and spirits of our sisters and brothers. We ask that as we drink the juice you would begin new growth that will bear much fruit. Amen.

# A Litany of Acknowledgment and Confession

*Based on Mark 15:15-20*
*By Cindy Hines Kurfman*

Leader:   So Pilate, wishing to satisfy the crowd, released
Barabbas for them; and after flogging Jesus, he hand-
ed him over to be crucified.

All:   We acknowledge our sisters and brothers who, like
Jesus, have been whipped and punished, victims of
another's crime, while the guilty party has been set
free.
We confess that we, the crowd, have often been
satisfied with this "disciplining" and have let the
abuse continue.

Leader:   Then the soldiers led him into the courtyard of the
palace (that is, the governor's headquarters) and they
called together the whole cohort.
They clothed him in a purple cloak; and after twisting
some thorns into a crown, they put it on him.
And they began saluting him, "Hail, King of the
Jews!"

All:   We acknowledge those among us who have been
mocked in front of their peers, who have had every
aspect of their lives criticized, and their words
distorted—all for having told the truth about their
abuse.
We confess that we have been among these
disbelievers.

Leader:   They struck his head with a reed, spat upon him, and
knelt down in homage to him.

All:   We acknowledge our brothers and sisters who, like
Jesus, have been struck on the head. Some have
endured bruises. Some have been disgraced with spit.
We confess that our belief in nonviolence has not
always carried over into our homes.
We also acknowledge that there are those who in
public feign kindness toward our sisters and brothers
while privately humiliating and abusing them.

Leader: After mocking him, they stripped him of the purple cloak and put his own clothes on him.

All: We acknowledge those among us who by force have been stripped of their clothes and childlikeness.
We acknowledge that they rightfully deserve to be clothed with respect.
We confess that we have failed to view our abused sisters and brothers as innocents.

Leader: Then they led him out to crucify him.

All: We acknowledge our sisters and brothers who have died from the results, either direct or indirect, of their abuse.
We confess our complicity in their deaths by our secrecy and our denial.
God, open our eyes to see the abuse that surrounds us.
Open our mouths to name what we see.
Use our hands to heal our sisters and brothers. Open our hearts to feel their pain and love them in their journey to wholeness.
Grant us courage and strength and empowering love.
Amen

## Affirmation of Faith

*By Carolyn Holderread Heggen*

Group 1: We believe that beyond the violence,
Group 2: there can be love;
Group 1: That beyond the despair,
Group 2: there can be hope;
Group 1: That beyond the torment,
Group 2: we will find rest;
Group 1: That beyond our brokenness,
Group 2: there can be healing;
Group 1: That beyond our agony,
Group 2: we will find joy.
All: Oh, God, transform our disbelief and gently carry us from darkness to light.

## A Prayer in Three Parts

*Inspired by Isaiah*
*By Joyce Munro*

### I

Because you are acquainted with grief and anger, dear God,

Hear our sobs

for children abused and neglected by those they trust;
for girls and women violated by men,
for wives taught to submit and sacrifice until their spirits have
    been deadened;

for boys and men treated as objects,
for husbands taught to believe they are not spiritual beings
    unless they dominate women and children.

Hear our outrage

at parents, relatives, pastors, youth sponsors, church leaders,
    teachers, mentors, and counselors

who have exploited those in their care.

Oh, God of grief and anger,
Comfort, comfort your people,
Do not forsake us.

### II

Because you are the everlasting God, Creator of the universe,

Give birth to us anew;
Leave nothing undone;
Purge shame, overturn greed,
Ransom our sins of relationship;
And show us how to love.

Oh, everlasting God, Creator of the wide world,
Let each of us know we are yours.

**III**

Because you are the God of gathering,

Shine out!
Shine out
And bestow your Spirit upon us;

Rain righteousness,
Even in the wilderness of our waywardness,
That we may blossom forth;

Plant justice on earth
As you promised,
Without breaking the bruised reed;

In the arms of your grace,
Hold us,
Through deep water or scorching flame,
Mercifully hold us;
Let no one be squandered
or lost.

Amen, Amen, Amen.

## Out of the Depths

*Compiled by Ann Campbell*

Psalms 102:1-2, 4-5: Psalms 109:29-31; Psalms 129:1-2;
130:1 (NASB)

Leader:   Hear my prayer, O Lord!
          Let my cry for help come to you.
Group:    Out of the depths
          I have cried to you, O Lord.
Leader:   Many times they have persecuted me
          from my youth up.
Group:    Do not hide thy face from me in the day
          of my distress.
Leader:   My heart has been smitten like grass
          and has withered away.
Group:    Indeed, I forget to eat my bread.
          Because of the loudness of my groaning,
          my bones cling to my flesh.
Leader:   I lie awake,
          I have become like a lonely bird on a housetop.
Group:    Many times they have persecuted me
          from my youth up.
          Yet they have not prevailed against me.
Leader:   Let my accusers be clothed with dishonor,
          And let them cover themselves with their own shame
          as with a robe.
Group:    With my mouth I will give thanks abundantly
          to the Lord;
          And in the midst of many I will praise him.
          For the Lord stands at the right hand of the needy,
          To save them from the ones who judge their souls.

# Prayer for the Smallest

*By Joyce Munro*

Our gracious creative God,
We hold up the most fragile ones among us now
for your attention;

We beseech for these your tenderest love and mercy,
for they have suffered
at the hands of those who fed and taught them
and have fallen like sparrows in the grass.

Yet we, too,
your eye on earth, Word made flesh,
have committed many tragedies in their regard:

> We have required silence
> as their expression of peace,
> And when they have broken silence,
> too often we have moved to protect ourselves,
> sometimes even called their truths, lies.
> We have used them for our own gain,
> For we are tempted to power over the weak.
> We snatch away their innocence
> and heap on them shame that belongs to us.

These are our sins toward the weakest;
We confess them
and ask now for your healing touch
on them and us.

Let the smallest thrive
In innocence and beauty;
Feed them,
Teach them clarifying anger,
and restore them to their dignity.

Let us make the journey through
the valley of our own shame and fragility,
Let the weak show us the path,
regardless of the immediate cost to our serenity.

Gracious creative God,
Mother the smallest secret ones in each of us,
until we can cherish them ourselves.
Amen.


Jeanette Gascho writes:

> I usually don't like litanies—they feel to me like someone is putting words in my mouth. This one is designed so members of the congregation can choose which words they want to speak.
>
> I envision this litany being used in a service which emphasizes how we are all part of the problem of sexual abuse and all contribute to keeping survivors from healing. This is a confession of our action and inaction. I see it being used in a service where there is opportunity for making new commitments to walk with the abused in redemptive ways.
>
> Directions: The congregation should be given time to read through the litany in silence, to decide which statements are true for them and to mark lines they wish to read in the corporate reading. The people who read a given statement are then confessing their own sin. If there is silence, the leader reads out loud. These confessions are directed to the survivors in the congregation. Whether or not the survivors have been identified publicly, they are in the congregation. They will hear.

## Litany of Confession

*By Jeanette M. Gascho*


- I have doubted your story because abuse seems like the currently popular thing to dredge up; I've thought you were just getting on the bandwagon too.
- I have wondered if you were lying to get attention.
- I've wondered if you were lying to hurt other people.
- I didn't believe your story because of the kind of person you are.
- I didn't understand that you are the kind of person you are in part because of your story.

- I have wished this whole abuse thing would go away.
- I have wished you would stop talking about it.
- I wanted it all to be over; I didn't want this to happen in my church.
- I have hoped that if we don't talk about it, then it won't be so bad.
- I have wished you would leave what's passed in the past.
- I'm tired of talking about abuse; let's talk about something else for awhile.
- I have felt this should be talked about in private, not public.
- I have avoided meetings or services when I knew abuse would be the topic.

- I didn't understand why you wanted everyone to know.
- I didn't understand why you wanted to be anonymous.
- I thought about your pain, and I hurt for you, but I didn't tell you.
- I withdrew from you because I didn't know how to treat you.
- I have asked you how you are, but I didn't want an honest answer.

- I have been angry at you for bringing it up now.
- I have thought that maybe in some ways you deserved what happened.
- In my heart I have accused you of bringing it all on yourself.
- I have been secretly jealous of all the attention you're getting.

- I have assumed I understood what you are going through.
- I have assumed I know what you need to heal. I didn't ask what you need from me.
- I have not protected you in the ways you have asked to be protected.
- I have not given you the gift of my memories that could help fill in your memory gaps.
- I have compared your journey to the journey of others to see how you measure up.
- I have asked your family and friends about you rather than speaking directly to you.

- I have not understood that the pain you have suffered affects your whole life; I have wanted you to keep it separate.

- I have not written a letter to church publications supporting the printing of articles about abuse.
- I have not encouraged church leaders to learn more about the issue.
- I have not offered financial assistance to you when you needed it to get counseling.
- I have pushed you to make the same church commitments you made last year; I have made it hard for you to say "no."
- I have not examined my own life to see how I have helped perpetuate abuse.

All:   Merciful God, hear our confession and forgive us our sins committed against our abused sisters and brothers. Make us vessels of your healing and grace, of your love and compassion. Amen.

## Remembrance and Confession

*By Elsie K. Neufeld*

Our Creator God:
You have called us into being,
breathed life into each one of us,
molded us in your image.
Potter of holy clay,
You have fashioned genders:
male and female
Painted skins and hair:
black, white, yellow, red.
Colored eyes: brown, blue,
green, and gray.
Oh, holy Father Mother God
You call us "my people"
give each of us a name.
You call the church "the bride of Christ"

The bride of Jesus, your Son!
And yet. And yet.
We are anything but pretty!
Cheeks blushed perhaps, but not with joy.
With shame. With shame.
Do you really want us?
We are a broken people
Our needs are great, our sins countless.
Our wants guide our behavior
the love we offer, conditional at best.
We hide our guilt,
glue masks to our faces.
We are betrayers and deniers,
liars and thieves,
offenders, abusers.
Blind! Deaf! Dumb!
Truth is our victim
and grace, your grace,
deformed by our shallow definition.
And yet. And yet.
Your proposal does not die:
"Come to me, all you who are weary and burdened, and I will
give you rest."

## Acceptance and Request for Guidance

*By Elsie K. Neufeld*

Oh, most gracious God,
we accept your invitation
We will be your bride
and body here on earth.
Sisters and brothers,
family of God. Holy Kingdom.
Spirit of God, come close;
Teach us how to do this work!
Inspire and strengthen!
Grant patience. Plant love in our hearts.

Water us with grace and compassion,
With your light shine clarity on our confusion.
Paint redemption on our faces,
Hang rainbows on our darkened souls,
Shade our heads with the shadow of the cross.
Saturate our minds with Christlike images,
Build your kingdom in us, through us, around us.
Feed us mercy, so that we may be a feast for those in famine.
Be near, Lord. Be near!
Move in our midst, Giver of Life
Lover of all.

## Jesus, Model of Redemption

*By Elsie K. Neufeld*

Jesus, Son of God, Son of man and woman.
You taught us well,
you showed us how to live.
And yet. And yet.
We falter.
Deny injustice, hurt instead of heal,
use hands as weapons. Choose faithlessness
instead of loyalty. Choose security instead of risk.
Smile instead of weep. Choose indifference in the face of
    violence.
Jesus, Son of God,
Forgive us for we know not what we do.

## God's People, Life Givers

*By Elsie K. Neufeld*

Mother Father God
As you have called Christ back to life,
so too we claim your promise to give us life,
abundant life.
We gather together as your people,

to call each other to renewal.
We want to love each other
as you love us.
We want to stand in the place of the victim,
to cry for justice and healing
for the battered, abused, and neglected.
We want to pray with them, for them,
and in their stead,
as our Lord and Savior Christ once did.
All-knowing God,
Open our eyes and ears,
loosen our tongues,
so that we might be attuned
and responsive to the victims in our families,
churches, and communities around us.
As we commit ourselves to be present for the victim,
Give us wisdom to deal redemptively,
to walk alongside, to share the heavy burden.
To be agents of growth and change
To clothe the victim in dignity.
To grant the victim personhood and respect.
To know when to stand back
in order to give room to heal,
to be a friend, not a rescuer;
to be a guide, not a director;
to be and do as our Lord and Savior Christ would.
Give us courage to walk into the darkness,
to seek the oppressed,
to find the wounded and faint-hearted,
as you have done for us through Jesus Christ.
Help us to be as stars on a summer night in pathways
darkened by the sinful violence of others.
As the sun lights the day and the moon the night,
so too we want to shine your light
into the lives around us.
We love you, Father Mother God.
Help us to be like you—
Wounded healers, givers of grace,

lovers of justice, children of truth,
people of God.

## Prayer

*By Nancy S. Lapp*

God of the Broken and Hurting,
  we come to you because
  you know what it's like
  to be rejected and abused,
  to suffer unjustly, innocently.
  You know the needs of those who suffer
  because of physical, emotional, sexual abuse.

God of Healing and Blessing,
  our hearts cry out
  for your mercy and love
  to heal our woundedness.
  Touch the child within us
    who needs to know love and acceptance,
    who can teach us how to play and enjoy life.
  In your mercy give courage
    to face painful memories
    to journey toward wholeness.
  Bring healing
    to damaged self-confidence
    to battered self-esteem
    to the ego with inadequate boundaries.
  Teach us to trust in appropriate and healthy ways.

Forgiving, Merciful God,
  you know the cost of forgiveness,
  the difficulty of forgiving.
  Especially you know
  how hard it is to forgive violence
  to one's own body and soul.
  Give us courage to be angry
    at injustice done to us,

courage to grieve what we have lost,
courage to heal,
    to let go of the hatreds that bind us.

Spirit God,
    touch our spirits
        with your healing love
        with your wisdom and courage
        with your compassion.
    Give us hope.

God-of-all-Life,
    raise us to new life
    to new ways of relating
    show us your unconditional Love
    help us to love ourselves as you love us
    and to love others as we love ourselves.

May your Blessing and Healing rest upon us. Amen.

## Litany of Commitment

*By Joyce Munro*

| | |
|---|---|
| All: | We commit ourselves to a world, to homes, and to churches, <br> Where we attempt to weave whole cloth again— |
| Leader: | Where those still so close to God, <br> our little children, <br> can weave in as high as they can reach, <br> their shimmering white and gold yarns; |
| Men: | And women lovingly restore to the cloth <br> their red and purple, <br> threads of their passion, <br> threads of their power; |
| Women: | And men weave in the green and orange <br> of earth colors, <br> all the strength of their tears, <br> their tenderness in them; |

Men:    And from those cast aside
for lack of perfect bodies, articulate minds,
the weaving in of rainbow yarn
for their deep capacity to have hope;

Women:    And from those who have used
their power wrongly,
but have changed—
pink for creativity,
yellow for transformation.

Men and Women Over Sixty:
Let us elders and crones bring ancient hues
to the weaving cloth—
brown, rose, and violet—
our sense of all that will pass,
our sense of all that will come;

Women:    While we who have had our boundaries
of self ravaged,
let us add stunning black,
our color dignifying the others;

Teens and Children:
Let this whole cloth include
that which is not always known as thread—
feathers,
grass,
seeds, and
fur
for resplendent mystery that is each living thing.

Leader:    And let us ask the great I AM
who intuits each heart
who knows star space
to draw blue through the warp
blessing upon blessing
blue upon blue
until there is whole cloth again.

All:    (With bells, clapping, and stomping) AMEN!

# Chapter 10

# Preventing Sexual Abuse

My practical farmer friend, Clif Kenagy, tells a story (which has been told in various forms) of a man who was working in his garden one day when he saw a desperate person being swept down the nearby river.

Tossing his rake aside, the gardener ran to the riverbank, pulled the drowning man from the turbulent waters, and administered successful mouth-to-mouth resuscitation. Several days later another drowning person floated by, then another. In subsequent weeks additional drowning victims periodically came down the river.

Each time the gardener tried to rescue them. Sometimes he was able to revive them on the spot but other times he had to rush them to the nearest hospital. Sometimes they survived but not infrequently they died before reaching the hospital.

Realizing that more victims could be saved if medical facilities were closer, the good gardener began an ambitious fundraising campaign to collect money to build a hospital on his land. Funds were raised and the hospital built. Many drowning victims pulled from the waters were revived in the fine new hospital.

A decade passed and a grand anniversary celebration was planned. Dignitaries came from near and far to honor the gardener and his visionary, successful hospital. During the festivities, a small boy came up to the gardener with one question: "Has anyone ever checked to see what's going on upstream?"

Because the effects of sexual abuse are so severe and destructive, efforts must continue both to help past victims recover and to prevent further abuse. Sexual abuse *can* be prevented. It will not, however, be an easy task. The prevention of abuse will require a radical transformation of the way we think about the family and God's intentions for the way men, women, and children live together.

To prevent sexual abuse, we must reconsider our basic beliefs about femaleness and maleness. Working to prevent sexual abuse will require courage, stamina, and the mobilization of our best spiritual resources. We aren't battling mere bad habits or annoying systems: in a very real sense we are confronting the powers of evil and darkness.

**1. *The church must challenge patriarchy*.** Sexual abuse may no longer be considered a mere personal problem or individual tragedy. Abuse must instead be seen as common, normative, and frighteningly logical in a patriarchal society. The church must creatively challenge the assumption that patriarchy represents the best and only way to live in relationship. It must fight the belief that God intended for men to dominate women and children.

Congregations should be places where people experience shared power, where they learn new models of partnership. The church should provide settings in which women, men, and children together discuss ideas and make plans. The church should be a place where respect and position are not determined by worldly measures of gender and power but by kingdom standards of love, spirituality, and giftedness.

The world will continue to elevate the man with the most degrees, power, and influence. But the church must constantly make sure it uses different criteria for making decisions, choosing leaders, and living together.

**2. *Use appropriate language*.** If congregations are to challenge patriarchy and stop abuse they must pay attention to the language used to talk about women, men, and God. *Androcentric* language—language which focuses on "man," is not only inaccurate. It is damaging and dangerous. Language has the power to define *a* reality and then names it as *the* reality. Language encodes a reality, then reinforces it. Androcentric language denies women and women's experience. It communicates to males and females, adults and children, that men are the norm, the standard, the most important.

Cultural tendencies to overlook the important feminine contribution to humanity are intensified by our English language. In our vocabulary, women are derived from men—fore*fathers*, *man*kind, wo*man*, fe*male*. Women's significant and unique contributions are undermined, for example, when work is described as "manpower" and products of labor as "manmade."

I know people who are perplexed and irritated with women who say they don't feel included when male language is used. The insistence that people use accurate language (if you mean "men" say "men" but if you mean both men and women say "men and women" or "people") is seen as petty by some. But if a woman says she doesn't feel included by androcentric language, why argue with her or try to explain that she really is included? She either feels included or doesn't. Logical explanations won't change her reality. Just because *some* women say they can identify with male language doesn't mean *all* women can.

I have asked groups of children to draw a picture of the word "forefathers" or "mankind." When I ask them why they drew all males in their picture, they seem confused. One indignant little girl exclaimed, "You didn't *say* to draw any women!"

The use of "man" and "mankind" as generic terms communicates to both females and males, in subtle but powerful ways, that male is the norm and that females are seen and evaluated in relationship to the male. Male generic terms disempower women and make them invisible. Language which ignores woman's reality and turns her invisible makes it less likely that she will recognize her own needs for health and safety as legitimate (Adams, 1992). An "invisible" woman is less likely to be able to protect herself and her children from an abusive man.

Man-centered language damages males by perpetuating in them the erroneous, evil belief that they are more important than women. It communicates that men are the norm, the reality around which the world, women, and children must move. It instills deeply in males the unchristlike belief that the male outlook, needs, and reality take precedence.

The Bible uses many different names and images for God. The parables of Jesus reflect a balance of male and female imagery remarkable even by today's standards. Nonetheless, the church has used primarily masculine images and names for God. If you doubt this, ask a group of children to draw a picture of God. Probably they will draw a character that looks a lot like Santa Claus, Grandpa, or their favorite bearded old man.

Both males and females have internalized a connection between masculinity and divinity. They don't make this same connection between femininity and the divine. This appears related to the names we give God. It is reinforced by the fact that Jesus was a man, the twelve disciples who formed the inner circle and get included in most artistic renditions of the disciples were men, and the angels named in the Bible all have masculine names. The connection between God and masculinity is further strengthened by a long history of female exclusion from positions of leadership in the church and the largely male leadership of the church.

When females have internalized a strong connection between masculinity and the divine, it makes it difficult to stand strong against a male's demands. A survivor says, "I'm not quite sure how it happened, but when I was a little girl God and my daddy were all mixed up into one. They were both very powerful and very much in charge of me and my world. I couldn't hide or run away from either of them. With both I was totally powerless. I knew both would have the final word; they'd get back at me in the end if I defied them.

"I'm over fifty years old and I still visualize my father when I sing certain hymns about God. I'm starting to understand how this confusion has damaged my relationship with God. But it feels awkward trying to think of God as something other than a father. There's not much support for trying out other images of God."

Congregations that are serious about preventing sexual abuse and challenging the destructive effects of patriarchy must carefully examine their language. The language we use to talk about women and men will influence our beliefs about men and women and will color our relationships. The language we use to describe and name God has a profound impact on our experience of and ability to enter a loving, transforming relationship with the divine and with each other.

**3. *Name the sin of abuse.*** Another important step for congregations which wish to prevent abuse is naming the sin of abuse. Carol Adams (1992) correctly observes that while silence is the opposite of speaking, denial is the opposite of naming. We have been too gentle when speaking of the church's *silence* regarding sexual abuse in Christian homes and churches. It is more correct to speak of the church's *denial* of the problem. It is appropriate to confess that our denial has further wounded victims and encouraged abusive behavior. "As long as violence is both invisible and unnamed, it is tacitly condoned" (Adams, 1992, p. 4). Our silence not only immobilizes the victims but allows and encourages continued abuse by perpetrators.

In the Bible, naming is a powerful act of dominion. In Genesis 2:19-20, Adam exercises his dominion over the animals by naming them. In 2 Kings 23:34, the victorious Pharaoh Neco renamed the conquered Judean king. Likewise, in naming the sin of abuse, churches can take one important step toward conquering this evil.

Courageous pastors among us who have dared name abuse from the pulpit have been shocked by the result. Most tell of many victims coming to them afterward to share stories of personal violation. Many carried their abuse as a secret wound in their heart for decades. Once the sin was publicly named, victims felt permission had been granted to share their story with someone in the church. Unnamed, abuse can not be healed or stopped. Adequately named, we can begin to exert dominion over this evil.

Worship services provide an important forum in which to

name the sin of abuse. Public worship is usually the setting where most people are gathered. Worship is an important element in the life of the congregation. In sermons pastors should name the sin of abuse and explain why it violates God's will for families. The sermon can communicate that sexual abuse will not be considered a "woman's problem" any more but a central concern of the entire congregation.

Pastors should state clearly that abuse will not be tolerated. They should urge both victims and perpetrators to talk to someone in the congregation. Church leaders should state clearly and frequently that what happens in homes is a concern of the church: "Sexual abuse is a sin and if it is happening among us it is our business."

As has already been suggested, worship should include prayers, liturgies, and responsive readings which name abuse and acknowledge the pain of victims. Prayers and sermons should offer hope for the healing of victims, perpetrators, and their families.

**4. *Dispel the notion that what happens in homes is private and no one else's business.*** The message that congregational members are concerned about and care for each other, regardless of family boundaries, must be clearly communicated.

Unfortunately, this prescription assumes a congregation will be healthier than its individual families, perhaps and this is often not the case. Many congregations are dysfunctional, don't function in healthy ways. Some congregations are as dysfunctional or more so than their dysfunctional members and families. Such congregations are frequently seduced into thinking that by making dysfunction in individual members or families the business of the entire congregation, they have promoted health. Instead, they may have simply succeeded in deepening the problem or spreading it more widely through the congregation.

Thus congregations must keep a watchful, honest eye on their own health. They must exercise extreme care before assuming they can intervene helpfully in lives of dysfunctional congregational members. But once congregations have worked at this rigorous self-assessment, they may be able to promote health in a variety of ways.

One way congregations can foster family health is through premarital counseling sessions which include clear teaching that the congregation cares passionately about the marriage. The congregation can at this time make a commitment to walk with a couple through the good times and the bad.

The engaged couple should understand the legitimate concern of the church that all people in the family—husband, wife, and any future children—be nurtured, cherished, and safe from emotional, physical, and sexual abuse. The couple should be told that if either spouse or any of their children ever feel unsafe in the family, the church wants to be informed. This is so the church can aid the family in finding help to change the behaviors and protect family members.

The couple should be encouraged to find other people in the congregation with whom to share sexual or marital problems which arise between them. The pastor may encourage couples to include in the marriage vows they make before the congregation and God the promise that they will not do violence to each other or their children.

Children need opportunities within the congregation to talk about fears or concerns they may have. Parents need to know that in the body of believers we share our joys and sorrows. This includes positive family experiences and also events which demoralize and wound us. Parents and children need to be reminded regularly that we don't hide painful things from each other but work together within the congregation to develop attitudes and behaviors which nurture people.

Men need to be reminded that the home isn't their private castle and children and wives aren't subjects for men to control. Everyone needs to be reminded that it is undesirable to keep secrets which hurt and destroy people's bodies and spirits.

**5.** *Communicate that the pastoral staff is trained and willing to intervene in abusive families.* Everyone on the pastoral staff should receive training to know how to intervene effectively with abusive families. They should know the reporting required by abuse laws. They should also have access to information about local resources and should understand emergency intervention strategies. If the pastoral staff is all male, choose a lay woman as contact person for members with abuse issues. Some women and young girls will not talk to a man about abuse concerns. Consider adding a woman to the pastoral staff.

**6. Examine the church's theology for teachings associated with abuse.** We need our theologians to help us consider which teachings may contribute to abuse. Are there religious values and teachings which may make people more vulnerable to abuse? Has emphasis on the value of suffering, obedience, and quick forgiveness been related to abuse? Have our teachings about submission somehow led to patterns of family life which make women and children vulnerable? Has the notion of mutual submission been understated among us? Any teaching which is not good news for both women and men, both children and adults, is surely a distortion of the gospel and must be reconsidered.

**7. Expect leaders to model exemplary sexual lives.** Because of their high calling, high visibility, and high influence among us, pastors and other church leaders should be expected to live godly lives. When they violate Christian standards of appropriate behavior, the church must call them to accountability, repentance, and changed behavior. Expectations for the behavior of leaders should be clearly stated. Procedures for reporting pastoral misconduct should be understood. Guidelines for disciplining unethical leaders and evaluating their future involvement with the church should be clearly formulated and followed.

**8. Get members informed about and involved in issues related to sexual abuse.** Study groups and other Christian education settings can be used to share basic information about abuse and its prevention. Placing books in the library or on tables in the back of the church building can be a nonthreatening way for people to learn more about sexual abuse. Some churches have made these resources available without people needing to check them out or sign their names.

Once members become informed about sexual abuse, it is more likely they will work to prevent it. A pastor friend recently enlightened concerning abuse said, "You can claim ignorance only up to the time you learn about abuse. Subsequently, the 'I didn't know' excuse won't fly."

Encourage members to get involved as volunteers with community resources which support victims and families. Consider using congregational money to establish funds for helping members get abuse counseling and to support organizations working against abuse. By investing congregational time and money, members not only become more intensely involved but realize that the church is serious in its commitment to working against abuse.

9. *Empower women to become emotionally strong and self-respecting.* Ending abuse requires that women be empowered to become emotionally strong and self-respecting. When a woman sees herself as having personal power and options in life, she will be less inclined to put up with a violent, abusive husband. When a woman believes she is a wonderful child of God, created in the image of the divine, she will be less likely to condone violence against herself and her children.

When mothers have some sense of control over the way their lives are going, when they are self-respecting and emotionally strong, it is more likely children will respect them and see mothers as allies in their protection. Thus daughters will be more inclined to report abuse to their mothers. This is *not* to imply that mothers are to blame for fathers' abuse. It is instead to say that anything that can be done to empower women will be an important step toward prevention.

10. *Use congregational influence to fight pornography and other media which eroticize violence.* Ours is a culture which increasingly experiences and depicts violence of males toward females and children as sexually stimulating. Many popular movies, television shows, and magazines portray male sexual violence as acceptable and attractive.

Pornography isn't bad because it is sexual. It is bad because it is violent and because it degrades people. It isn't dangerous because it is sexual but because it communicates to men that women and children are objects to be used for men's sexual pleasure. It is bad because it frequently depicts violence against women as erotically exciting. Pornography which depicts children in sexual ways may communicate that children are appropriate, desirable sexual partners and may put children at increased risk of victimization.

**11. *Become advocates of children*.** The congregation must communicate clearly and in many settings and ways its opposition to violence against children. When violence does occur, the child's safety and well-being must be the immediate and primary concern for the church. Children need to know that their efforts to resist victimization will be supported.

Congregations should work to strengthen community protective services for children. They should support school programs which educate children about abuse and should work for vigorous enforcement of laws prohibiting abuse. Sunday school teachers and youth workers need training to detect signs of abuse. They should know procedures for reporting to authorities indications of violence to children. Children can only be as strong and effective in their own defense as the adults who stand beside them.

**12. *Educate children to recognize and report abuse*.** Children need to understand what sexual abuse is. They need to know that even people they love and trust may try to abuse them. It is important not to unduly frighten children. But for their self-protection, children must understand abuse—a real danger for at least one third of today's children. To expect parents in incestuous families to alert children to these dangers is like hoping the fox will warn the chickens of furry danger in the hen house.

Children need to be taught actions they can take if someone, even a parent, tries to abuse them. If abuse does happen, they need to be taught to report to someone in the church that they are being hurt. They need to know they must keep telling people until someone believes them and helps them to safety.

In a comfortable congregational setting, all children need to participate in discussions about "good touch" and "bad touch." They need to talk about the difference between surprises and secrets and how you know when to tell someone about something that is happening to you even if your parent has told you not to tell. Children need help understanding that while the Bible says that children are to obey their parents, the biblical command for obedience is conditional: "Children, obey your parents *in the Lord,* for this is right" (Eph. 6:1).

Children need a safe place to talk about things parents might ask them to do that Jesus wouldn't want them to do. They need opportunities to talk about things that didn't seem right that they were asked to do in the past by parents or someone in authority.

13. *Call both males and females of all ages to responsible, healthy sexual attitudes and behaviors.* The church must communicate its belief in the importance and goodness of human embodiment and teach that sexuality is an intrinsic dimension of human life. Members must understand that the church cares as much about their sexual attitudes and behaviors as about their devotional life. They must also know that sexuality issues *are* the business of the church. Members will be held accountable for what they do with their bodies and to other people's bodies. Chapter 11 discusses ways congregations can assist members to grow in responsible and joyful sexuality.

14. *Encourage and provide models of healthy male socialization.* As has been discussed, males have traditionally been taught that being a man means not being like the primary caretaker, most often the mother. Male identity has thus become a negative identity. The church should hold up positive, Christlike qualities for boys and men to model.

Congregations would do well to encourage nonabusive men to become more intimately involved in the caretaking of children. Increased contact with a caregiving father would help developing boys to associate nurturing qualities with masculinity. In addition, as men gain opportunities to become active in children's nurture, they are more likely to be defenders of children's well-being.

Men may come to understand how deprived they have been by cultural lies which tell them that a primary manly way to express caring and seek closeness is through sexual activity. In caring for children, men may learn to enjoy deeply affectionate relationships which have no sexual component.

Congregations can model and support social changes which encourage and allow men to give up their destructive, heavy burden of always needing to be in control and strong. In congregational matters, men need opportunities and encouragement to allow women to participate in decision making.

All people in the congregation need to learn to be in partnership together. Congregations need to provide settings where women and children's voices are heard and their reality shared—and men listen to that reality. When men assume *their* reality is the only one, they need to be called to accountability.

Congregations would do well to encourage men to develop close friendships with other men. When men learn to be intimate and honest with male friends, not only are their own lives enriched but also those of the women and children around them. While men have expected women to do much of the emotional work in relationships, men must be given opportunities and impetus to develop these skills for themselves.

Men's retreats and small groups can provide safe settings in which men may feel free to disclose the secrets of their souls and the longings of their hearts. These settings may encourage the development of close friendships between men, in which men may at last be free to give up pretending strength which they may not feel.

The church must communicate to boys and men that they are precious and valuable, not for what they do or achieve, but just for what they are—wonderful children of God. The church must challenge cultural messages which equate masculinity with aggressive, controlling behaviors and emotional repression.

Jesus provides a model for a countercultural way of being a man. In him churches can find a life enhancing model of masculinity expressed in gentle, tender, nurturing ways. Jesus provides a model for being male in relationship with children and women which calls out the best in all, which celebrates and honors the equal humanity and worth of all people. May it be so among us, Jesus' followers.

## Chapter 11

# Congregational Role in Developing Healthy Sexuality

Ours is a society obsessed with sex. Ours is a sexually saturated culture. Sexual images and messages bombard us from billboards and radio, from magazines and religious telebroadcasts. Sex is used to sell everything from Bibles to trucks. Cultural criteria for making sexual choices are only "Is it safe?" and "Is it pleasurable?"

The Christian community has never been able to count on society to establish standards of sexual behavior which reflect Christian values. But now, perhaps more than ever, the church needs to articulate and model a healthy, Christlike, countercultural understanding of sexuality. Before this can happen, however, the church must develop a biblical theology of the body and sexuality as a foundation on which members build healthier sexual lives.

## A Theology of Sexuality

A useful and appropriate theology of sexuality must address three issues: a biblical understanding of the body, God's intentions for sexuality, and ways to reverse the effects of the Fall in male-female relationships.

*A biblical understanding of the body.* We have already looked at unbiblical, unhealthy dualistic views of the human body which the Christian church has inherited. Current cultural notions of the body are different but equally destructive and unbiblical. Particularly for women, the body is elevated as the ultimate asset. Bizarre and self-destructive behaviors occur in an attempt to conform the female body to currently popular notions of thinness, youthfulness, and beauty.

Because women are told their value is tied to their physical beauty, many spend an enormous amount of time, energy, and money trying to meet current cultural standards of feminine beauty. They then deemphasize their development in other areas. It isn't that women are particularly fickle and vain; instead, they have been convinced by cultural lies that their worth lies in their approximation to ever-changing cultural standards of beauty.

A biblical theology of the body will affirm the goodness of our bodies as a special part of God's creation. It will consider the body the temple of the Holy Spirit and the place where the divine Word is made flesh. It will invite both men and women to claim the blessedness of being created in the image of God. A biblical theology will celebrate the rich variety of body shapes and sizes. It will deplore standards and devices of beauty which dehumanize, weaken, and restrict.

The divine incarnation of Jesus is an expression of the importance of the human body in the purposes of God. Our theology must invite both female and male to rejoice and delight in our body-selves. Our theology must help us embrace our sexuality as a part of good creation which reflects God's image in and among us (Gen. 1:27).

James Nelson (1978) observes that the way we think and feel about our bodies will find expression in the way we think and feel also about God, the world, and others. As a therapist sometimes working with perpetrators of sexual abuse, I have observed the dangers of thinking of body and spirit as separate. Such dualism results in an undue emphasis on person as spirit and a minimizes the importance of the things done by one's body to another's body.

When confronted with his sexually abusive behavior toward a young daughter, one devout Christian man said, "But that wasn't really me—it was my unredeemed carnal nature that did that to her." Repentance, healing, and changed behavior could only happen when he was able to accept that his body, with its inappropriate sexual urges, was as much a part of him as that part which led the congregation in worship, prayed, and fasted.

*God's intentions for sexuality.* A useful theology of sexuality must secondly address God's intentions for sexuality. Ours is a culture which has made an idol of sexual gratification. The primary Old Testament purpose for marriage and sexuality was to produce children. The Hebrews were God's chosen people, commanded to populate the earth. The biblical concept expressed in Genesis 2:24 of mates becoming "one flesh" involves more than the mere act of intercourse. Children bear the genes of both parents, in a marvelous way combining aspects of both parents in one flesh.

Beyond the procreative function of sexuality is the biblical notion of sexuality as the means for joyous expression of love. We have preferred to spiritualize the Song of Songs in the Bible. However, it may more accurately be seen as a graphic portrayal of romantic love and physical sensuality joined in sexual expression. Indeed, intimate sexuality can be a playful, exuberant expression of love. It can be a way for married couples to lay aside the heavy responsibilities of parenting and daily demands and celebrate life together.

In Ephesians 5:21-23, Paul speaks of the unifying function of sexual expression in marriage when he compares the husband-wife relationship to the union between Christ and the church. Family therapist and seminary professor Ross Bender observes that the union in one flesh of a husband and wife can overcome temporarily the tension in the female-male relationship as both experience a oneness. The human desire for sexual closeness expresses a deep longing for communion with each other and with God. Bender notes that what makes the relationship between Christ and the church and the relationship between wife and husband similar is the spiritual union, the uniting of mind, heart, values, intention, and destiny (Bender, 1982).

Humans do not need genital contact to be fulfilled and content. Married or single, however, we all must have love, affection, tender touch, and intimate communication to live creatively and happily. Celibate singles are no less sexual than their married counterparts. Instead of expressing their sexuality in overt genital contacts, sexuality for the celibate person will be expressed in affectionate relationships of deep friendship and care.

Both married and single people need to be in close relationships with females and males as we attempt to develop our divinely created nature in the image of God. We were created to be in community. Whether married or single we must have close contact with the opposite sex to develop our full humanity.

Unlike popular culture, which tends to view sexual expression as a mere physical, biological act, the church must view it in the context of spiritual, emotional, and moral considerations. Sexuality must always be integrated into the total life of the individual. We dare not compartmentalize our sexuality.

A holistic understanding will allow us to claim and enjoy our sexuality as an integral part of our lives, under the accountability and discipline of the Holy Spirit and other believers. If we do not embrace our sexuality, it becomes split off from us. It goes underground, affecting us in ways which we may not be aware. An underground sexuality is likely to operate without the constraints of personal and corporate scrutiny and guidance.

*Distortions caused by the Fall.* A third issue a theology of sexuality must address is distortions in female-male relationships caused by the Fall. Both the Old and New Testaments state that all persons are created in the image of God and given mutual dominion over the rest of creation. One result of the Fall is that man now has a tendency to distort shared dominion as permission for the domination of women. The positive, mutual interdependence that existed between man and woman before the Fall is now distorted.

As Mary Stewart Van Leewen (1990) observes, there is something akin to a congenital flaw in men which makes it easy for them to assume a right of domination over women. The command to love and cherish becomes distorted into desire and domination.

Biblical scholar Gilbert Bilezikian (1985) has noted the counterpart result of the Fall for woman. She will experience an unreturned longing for intimacy with man and her desire for community will be distorted by sin. Thus women will tend to avoid responsibility for accountable dominion in order to preserve even unhealthy relationships.

Women will be inclined to give too much in return for too little. They will tend to love without good judgment and thus continue their subordination to men. An examination of self-help books currently on the market indicates that indeed women are seeking to understand their propensity for becoming involved in destructive, entangled, abusive relationships.

In Jesus we see modeled a way of relating to women which goes back to the original intentions of creation. Jesus violated law and custom to treat women as human beings equal in worth to men. He refused to follow laws that dehumanized women, kept them in bondage, and sustained their inferiority and uncleanliness. Jesus demonstrated by his teachings and behavior a rejection of male rulership and a commitment to restoring women to the equal dignity and worth Eve held before the fall.

Jesus related to all people, including women, not on the basis of their socially defined roles, but on the basis of their common humanity. The gospels portray Jesus as reaching out even when it meant breaking degrading customs and laws. Jesus chose a woman to be the first witness of his resurrection even though at that time in history, a woman's word would not hold up in a court of law.

The church must follow the example of Jesus. It must call women and men to participate together in their full humanity. The church must aggressively challenge and eliminate language and practices which contradict the biblical teaching of female and male equality before God. The church must model mutuality and equality between males and females, for it is only in relationships of mutual respect, commitment, and equality that we can become the countercultural model of love and healthy sexuality our world so desperately needs. A clear and biblical theology of the body and sexuality will be an important step in this direction.

## Congregational Steps to Foster Healthy Sexuality

A biblical theology of the body and sexuality will give congregations a solid foundation on which to help members build healthy sexual attitudes and behaviors. Developing and explaining this theology may have eternal and practical results that will be more important in our lives than the church's theological stand on issues more commonly addressed.

Beyond articulating a proper body theology, there are other steps congregations can take to help foster healthy sexual attitudes and behaviors among members.

**1.** *Teach that sexuality is an important part of our communal life.* As individual Christians we have often been perplexed about how to regard and understand our body with its powerful sexual urges. We have been even more confused about what it means to be sexual beings called together into a spiritual relationship in the congregation.

The church has presented periodic sermons against the evils of adultery, homosexuality, and lust. It has faced occasional awkward instances of flagrant sexual misbehavior by members. But the inclination of the church has mostly been to act as though personal sexuality is not an appropriate congregational concern.

When congregations believe that how members live as sexual beings is as much a concern of the church as what members believe about other theological issues, individuals are helped to claim their sexuality as an essential part of their personhood. Then it becomes possible for sexual attitudes and behaviors to be under the accountability and discipline of the Holy Spirit and other believers.

When sexual matters are considered inappropriate concerns of the congregation, people find it easier to despise and disown sexual feelings. Unclaimed and unmonitored feelings may become dangerous and destructive.

**2. Provide settings where people talk about sexual issues.** Let's face it, sex education is going on all the time whether we acknowledge it or not. As children observe adults interacting, they are learning what it means to be sexual beings in relation to each other. As they watch who leads worship and who preaches, as they hear the language we use to name God, children are learning about sexual mutuality and equality. They are taking in our understanding of the relationship between femaleness, maleness, and the divine.

Sex education in any setting involves imparting information and developing attitudes. We know information doesn't necessarily affect behavior—attitudes do. Attitudes are learned primarily from parents. Unfortunately, many parents have a narrow vision of human sexuality and much anxiety around the subject.

Congregations can help parents or future parents acquire accurate information and develop positive, healthy attitudes about human sexuality. Premarital instruction classes may be the best opportunity congregations have to provide good sex education for adults and future parents. When children are born into the home, sex education begins immediately. During the early years of the child's life, the parents are the primary source of that education. But as a child approaches puberty, peers instead of parents may be the main source of sex information.

One task of adolescence is to consider and work through various ideologies so the young person can develop a personal, adult ethical sense. Just as at this time young people need to develop a spirituality separate from their parents, so too must they develop personal beliefs and attitudes about their sexual lives.

As adolescents necessarily pull away from their parents in this process, it becomes critical that other Christians within the congregation help them develop an understanding of sex within a broader context of theology and Christian lifestyle.

But it won't do to try to restrict our discussions of sexuality to its spiritual meanings. If we are going to get involved in the sex education of our young people, we must be prepared to talk about penises, vaginas, and orgasms. When parents have done their job of teaching comfortable, healthy attitudes toward sex, the congregation can build on this and help young people acquire accurate information and develop a distinctly Christian understanding of sexuality.

People other than parents and youth, however, need opportunities in the congregation to talk about sexuality and place it in the context of broader ethical-theological understandings. Adult single people need safe places where they can talk about the joys and frustrations of being both single and sexual beings. They need settings where they can be challenged and supported as they attempt to live faithful celibate lives and find appropriate ways of meeting their needs for intimacy and closeness. Elderly and handicapped persons need opportunities to discuss their special needs and challenges as sexual persons. People need opportunities within the congregation to explore what it means to be Christian and sexually attracted to persons of their same gender.

These are all issues of too great importance to be relegated to individual choice and decision making. We all need each other to understand what it means to be faithful and sexual, no matter what our age, special needs, or orientation.

*3. State clearly and model a sexual counterculture which reflects kingdom values.* Our culture, particularly since the "sexual revolution," patterns sexual standards on the individualistic and naturalistic model of human behavior. Our culture assumes that human nature operates in individuals independent of society and culture. Our society believes individuals have the right to seek sexual gratification apart from any secondary social convention such as marriage.

This societal model also assumes it is "natural" that people seek to satisfy their sexual passions and desires—the need for sex parallels the need for air, food, and water. Thus this need obviously must be met.

In our culture, sexual pleasure has been set up as an idol, a false god. As a church we must teach and model for our children the belief that Christ's call is to something greater than pleasure.

While we need to teach our children to appreciate and enjoy God's wonderful gift of sexuality, we must also teach them about God's intentions for sexuality. We must warn our children of the sorrow and destruction which result when people violate the divine plan for sexual interactions.

The congregation is a wonderful setting in which to teach and model the differences between the sexual behaviors of the world and among believers. Our culture may view sexual expression as a mere biological and physical act. But the church strives to integrate sex into the total life of people, where it must be seen in the context of spiritual and moral considerations.

**4. *Provide opportunities for members to use and enjoy their bodies in group settings.*** Outside of sexual expression and contact sports, our culture does not provide many opportunities for people, especially men, physically to touch each other. A male client once confessed that unless he was being sexual with his wife, violent with his children, or slapping his drinking buddies on the shoulder, he really didn't know how to touch people.

Congregations should provide settings where men may safely use their bodies to express feelings other than aggression or sex. Some people may need guidance to learn healthy ways of using their bodies to express tenderness and compassion. Asking people to put their hands on members being prayed for during the service may be one way. Asking people to join hands in prayer or to hug during the passing of the peace may be others. Coming forward to touch in blessing a member being commissioned for service or a child being dedicated provides opportunity for people to use their bodies as instruments of tenderness and love.

In planning worship, attempts should be made to teach members new ways of practicing the presence of God through movement, breathing, and using the body in prayer. Worship services too often have a lopsided emphasis on rational, intellectual expressions. A more active use of the body during worship such as moving to music and lifting or clapping hands may help bring appropriate passion and balance to our praise.

Having said all this, it is important for survivors to know that their touch boundaries will not be violated in church. This is critical for them to feel safe. Therefore, in planning and leading worship, we must discourage the expectation that everyone will touch in a particular way. People must have permission and a graceful way to refuse touching which violates their sense of safety and comfort.

Christian education committees would do well to acknowledge the body as an appropriate topic for study together. Congregations may want to offer classes in nutrition, relaxation, and wellness. Likewise, church members should have many opportunities to enjoy being body-selves together. Hymn sings, foot washing services, barn raisings (or some modern adaptations of this custom), quilting parties, service and work projects, volleyball games, and hikes are all ways in which members can interact in healthy bodily ways.

5. *Model healthy alternative ways of being female and male.*
Perhaps the most important step congregations can take to foster healthy sexual attitudes and behaviors is to model Christlike ways of being together as males and females. This book has already explored damage done to men and women in this culture as they are taught certain behaviors and attitudes considered appropriate for males and females. In a culture which teaches that being masculine means being strong, aggressive, dominant and in control, congregations must work creatively and consciously to communicate and model a different way of being male.

Because boys learn that being masculine means not being like their mother, not being a "sissy," qualities associated with mothering—nurturance, tenderness, gentleness, and emotional responsiveness—tend to be repressed and belittled in males. When these qualities weaken, it becomes more likely that men will abuse instead of protect and nurture children.

Boys are bombarded with images and models of men who dominate, control their own emotions and other people, and touch mostly through sex. Boys have few models, however, of men being vulnerable, gentle, and tender. Therefore congregations must provide opportunities where males can develop their nurturing, tender qualities and where young boys can see countercultural models of masculinity.

Boys need to see men expressing affection and tenderness in relationships that do not involve sex, such as male to male friendships and nurturing interactions with children. They need to see men helping with meal preparations and serving food in the congregation. Boys need many opportunities to see Christian men responding with gentle touch, emotional warmth, and vulnerability to others.

Society tells girls and women that females are submissive, passive, docile, and dependent. These attitudes and behaviors make it less likely a female will protect herself from abuse. The church must call forth the divine in women, teaching them that they too are made in God's image.

Females who truly believe they, just as men, are created in God's likeness are more able to protect themselves and their children against violence and abuse. Females in the congregation need help to distinguish between relationships based on exploitation and those based on equality and mutual consent.

Within the congregation, women should be challenged to use leadership abilities and spiritual gifts. They should be encouraged to work toward healthy relationships with husbands, friends, and families. They should be affirmed as they clarify their own needs and longings and work within relationships to have those needs met just as they try to nurture others.

Males should be challenged to examine their lives and relationships for patterns and attitudes which reflect more the Fall than God's original intentions for humanity. They should be encouraged, within a supportive, safe congregational setting, to identify and confess behaviors which overpower, dominate, and control women. They should be challenged to identify, confess, and change ways they demean females and treat them as objects.

Members of the body of Christ must work creatively to learn ways of functioning in partnerships based on affirming diversity, mutual responsibility, gentleness, and strength that empowers not only men but women and children as well. Both men and women should work for relationships which reflect the male-female mutuality, equality, and complementarity portrayed in the Genesis creation account as God's intent for human relationships. When members become comfortable with their bodies and exhibit wholesome sexual attitudes and behaviors, new energy will characterize congregational worship and life together.

## *Epilogue*
# Dreaming Beyond the Gender War

A war is being waged. Humans have long been aware of the war; we have even made a cliché of it, calling it the "battle of the sexes." As everpresent as this war has been, it has often been easy to minimize it. Societies have taught their men and women that the tensions between them are just the way things are. Men must be men; women must be women. Any conflict is caused by the inability of men to claim their rightful role or of women to accept their appropriate place. Needed is simply better adjustment to age-old, patriarchal patterns of gender relationships.

Now, however, it is becoming more evident that the way things are isn't working. Many women are rising to claim the dignity, power, and equality so long denied them. They are demanding an end to the abusive patterns patriarchy has too often encouraged and which this book documents. On behalf of their own and their sisters' wounds, women are lighting candles, and they are taking the candles into the dark corners of church and society to reveal the atrocities that have been hidden there.

Some men are seeing that pressure to dominate women, children, even the entire world, has damaged men—and made them in turn wound others. These men are sensing the torment of their sisters. Even as they wince, they are accepting their complicity in the atrocities their sisters' candles are exposing. These men now see that they have been blind to the consequences of their assumption that women are theirs to lead, to control, to do with what they will. They have been blind to ways they have dehumanized women, making them not sisters but pets, property, even objects of torture.

But even many of these men are not finding it easy to know what it means to reach out to their sisters yet still be men. If they give up the ancient patterns of manhood bred into their very bones, what patterns will replace them? How will they know what it means to listen to their own inner male voice, rather than simply to the voices of women telling them how abusive they have been and what kind of men to be? Even these men, who see and grieve over the anguish they have helped inflict on women, sometimes feel angry at the loss of old guidelines for being men.

Then there are the men who want nothing to do with the notion that their ways of being men and relating to women must change. They are stockpiling weapons and digging trenches in hopes of vanquishing this uprising of women and soft, traitorous men. The old ways must be defended.

And so tensions mount and enmities deepen and the war goes on. There is probably no quick and simple way to end this war because so much is at stake. Much will need to be resolved, perhaps over generations, before true peace can be declared. Women will need convincing evidence that their personhood is respected and granted space for full expression. Men trained that manhood means dominating women (and indeed nearly everything else) will need to learn what it means still to be men—yet accept, support, and even celebrate women as full equals.

As inevitable as a period of war may be, however, we— Carolyn Holderread Heggen and Michael King—are writing this epilogue together because we dream of the peace beyond the war. We are writing as a woman and a man because we want to symbolize the potential for women and men to work together instead of against each other. We are writing as a woman and a man because we have caught hints—in our marriages, our friendships, and our own joint work as writer and editor of this book—of glory.

We dream that Isaiah's vision of glory (Isa. 11:6ff.) will apply even to men and women. We dream of a land of peace, where not only the wolf and the lamb but also women and men and girls and boys will together frolic. Though we have only begun to enter it, we have at least glimpsed the grandeur of the new terrain, still barely explored, beyond tragic gender warfare.

How might we all enter that strange but glorious land of healed gender relationships? Three steps, among others, may help us stumble onward. One step is *to transform the meaning of power.* Power as domination, as power-over, only perpetuates gender war. But power rooted in mutual respect can become power-with, power-in-relation, power shared among all rather than rationed among the few. As we learn to see all humans as joined in partnership, not divided into bosses and underlings, the dominators and the dominated, we will revolutionize child-rearing styles, marriages, and social organizations.

A second step is *to learn win/win arrangements.* We can cease playing a win-lose "zero-sum" game where you lose if I win—and we both end up hurt, because when someone loses no one truly wins. Women already well know the cost of being losers in the battle with men; they rightly want to win. Flipping the equation so men now become losers will only create a new cycle of bitterness. Instead we can all win. Your growth and mine can enhance each other.

Men and women can begin win/win relating by recognizing that all lose when some traits and privileges are reserved for one gender. Women lose when strength, power, and control are seen as male prerogatives. Men lose when tenderness, vulnerability, and emotion are deemed female gifts. But when traits are traded as needed, all win. We become new and larger human beings as we draw on a smorgasbord of possibilities rich beyond anything imaginable in traditional gender arrangements.

A third step is *to battle a common enemy instead of each other.* We are all, men and women, fragile beings who must stick together to fight evil, the loneliness of human existence, the dangers of our voyage through a fallen creation. Although humans often find unity in opposing a third party, let our union come not from making each other the third party but from together fighting the forces that fragment us.

As female writer and male editor, we tried, while producing this book, to practice the three steps we are preaching. We recognized we both had a right to power. Carolyn deserved the power to speak as she saw fit. Michael needed the power to shape the book according to the requirements of publishing and marketing a viable book.

Either of us could have tried to use our power to dominate the other. Then we both would have lost. If Carolyn had demanded that her wording be final, Michael's job would have been impossible. If Michael had squashed Carolyn's voice into a rigid framework, Carolyn's right to speak with integrity would have been violated.

Gradually we found a win/win approach. First Carolyn wrote as she saw fit. Next Michael edited as he saw fit. Then we conversed concerning the final text. We each held firm when we thought we must; we each gave ground when we thought we could do so with integrity; we each celebrated the outcome.

The going wasn't always easy. At times we were tempted to see the other as the enemy. Not yielding to temptation required frank letters, phone calls—and even one face-to-face interaction allowing us to intuit whether to offer mutual trust. As our relationship grew, however, we saw that our real enemies were sexual abuse, sexual sin, broken gender relationships. By together fighting such foes, we forged a union precious beyond words.

Peace between the sexes remains as much dream as reality. But we dream on, trusting that little by little God will transform the hints of glory men and women are even now experiencing with each other into candles brightening all the shadows of a sad and sin-shrouded globe.

—*Michael A. King, Philadelphia, Pennsylvania; and
Carolyn Holderread Heggen, Albuquerque, New Mexico*

# Bibliography

Adams, C. J. (1992). *Naming, Denial and Sexual Violence.* Manuscript submitted for publication.

Adorno, T. W., D. J. Levinson, E. Frenkel-Brunswik, and R. N. Sanford, (1950). *The Authoritarian Personality.* New York: Harper.

Allender, D. B. (1990). *The Wounded Heart: Hope for Adult Victims of Childhood Sexual Abuse.* Colorado Springs, Colo.: Navpress.

Allport, G. W. (1950). *The Individual and His Religion.* New York: Macmillan.

Augsburger, D. (1981). *Caring Enough to Forgive.* Scottdale, Pa.: Herald Press.

Bandura, A. (1977). "Self-efficacy: Toward a Unifying Theory of Behavioral Change." *Psychological Review, 84,* 191-215.

Bender, R. T. (1982). *Christians in Families.* Scottdale, Pa.: Herald Press.

Bell, A. and C. S. Hall (1976). "The Personality of a Child Molester." In M. S. Weinberg (ed.), *Sex Research: Studies from the Kinsey Institute.* Oxford: Oxford University Press.

Bilezikian, G. (1985). *Beyond Sex Roles: What the Bible Says About a Woman's Place in Church and Family.* Grand Rapids, Mich.: Baker Book House.

Blume, E. S. (1990). *Secret Survivors: Uncovering Incest and Its Aftereffects in Women.* New York: Ballantine Books.

Brewer, C. (1991). *Escaping the Shadows, Seeking the Light: Christians in Recovery from Childhood Sexual Abuse.* San Francisco: HarperCollins.

202

Brown, J. C. and C. R. Bohn (eds.). (1989). *Christianity, Patriarchy and Abuse; A Feminist Critique*. New York: Pilgrim Press.

Bullough, V., and Bullough, B. (1977). *Sin, Sickness, and Sanity: A History of Sexual Attitudes*. New York: The New American Library.

California Department of Mental Health, Office of Prevention. (1979). *In Pursuit of Wellness* (Report No. 108). San Francisco: Author.

Caputi, J. (1987). *The Age of Sex Crime*. Bowling Green, Ohio: Bowling Green State University Popular Press.

Carmody, D. (1979). *Women and World Religions*. Nashville: Abingdon.

Chodorow, N. (1974). "Family Structure and Feminine Personality." In M. Z. Rosaldo and L. Lamphere (eds.), *Woman, Culture and Society*. Stanford: Stanford University Press.

Christenson, L. (1970). *The Christian Family*. Minneapolis: Bethany Fellowship.

Clanton, J. A. (1990). *In Whose Image? God and Gender*. New York: Crossroad.

Coopersmith, S. (1967). *The Antecedents of Self-esteem*. San Francisco: W. H. Freeman.

Courtois, C. A. (1988). *Healing the Incest Wound*. New York: W. W. Norton and Company.

Creighton S. J. (1987). "Child Abuse in 1986." *Social Services Research, 16, 3,* 1-10.

Daly, M. (1975). *The Church and the Second Sex*. New York: Harper and Row.

Densen-Gerber, J. (1983). "Why Is There So Much Hard-Core Pornography Nowadays? Is It a Threat to Society or Just a Nuisance?" *Medical Aspects of Human Sexuality, 17,* 35.

Dinsmore, C. (1991). *From Surviving to Thriving: Incest, Feminism and Recovery*. Albany, N.Y.: State University of New York Press.

Dobson, J. (1970). *Dare to Discipline*. Glendale, Calif.: Regal Books.

Eisler, R. (1987). *The Chalice and the Blade: Our History, Our Future*. San Francisco: Harper and Row.

Enright, R. D., D. L. Eastin, S. Golden, I. Sarinopoulos, and S. Freedman, (1992). "Interpersonal Forgiveness Within the Helping Professions: An Attempt to Resolve Differences of Opinion." *Counseling and Values, 36,* 84-103.

Falwell, J., ed. (1981). *The Fundamentalist Phenomenon: The Resurgence of Conservative Christianity*. Garden City, N.J.: Doubleday.

Feierman, J. R., ed. (1990). *Pedophilia: Biosocial Dimensions*. New York: Springer-Verlag.

Feldmeth, J. R. and M. W. Finley, (1990). *We Weep for Ourselves and Our Children: A Christian Guide for Survivors of Childhood Sexual Abuse*. San Francisco: HarperCollins.

Finkelhor, D. (1984). *Child Sexual Abuse: New Theory and Research*. New York: The Free Press.

_____ (1986). *A Sourcebook on Child Sexual Abuse*. Newbury Park, Calif.: Sage Publications.

Fortune, M. M. (1983). *Sexual Violence: The Unmentionable Sin*. New York: The Pilgrim Press.

_____ (1989). *Is Nothing Sacred: When Sex Invades the Pastoral Relationship*. San Francisco: HarperCollins.

Fromuth, M. E. (1983). "The Long-term Psychological Impact of Childhood Sexual Abuse." Unpublished doctoral dissertation, Auburn University, Auburn, Ala.

Garbarino, J., and S. H. Stocking, (1980). *Protecting Children from Abuse and Neglect*. San Francisco: Jossey-Bass.

Gilligan, C. (1982). *In a Different Voice: Psychological Theory and Women's Development*. Cambridge, Mass.: Harvard University Press.

Goldstein, M. J., H. S. Kant, and J. J. Hartman (1973). *Pornography and Sexual Deviance*. Los Angeles: University of California Press.

Gothard, B. (1975). *Research and Principles of Life*. Oak Brook, Ill.: Institute in Basic Youth Conflicts.

Greven, P. (1990). *Spare the Child: The Religious Roots of Punishment and the Psychological Impact of Physical Abuse*. New York: Alfred A. Knopf.

Groth. N. A., and H. J. Birnbaum, (1978). *Adult Sexual Orientation and Attraction to Underage Persons. Archives of Sexual Behavior*, 7, 3, 175-181.

Gruber, K., and R. Jones, (1983). "Identifying Determinants of Risk of Sexual Victimization of Youth." *Child Abuse and Neglect*, 7, 17-24.

Hammer, R. F., and B. C. Glueck, Jr. (1957). "Psychodynamic Patterns in Sex Offenders: A Four-Factor Theory." *Psychiatric Quarterly* 31, 325-345.

Handford, E. R. (1972). *Me? Obey Him?* Murfreesboro, Tenn.: Sword of the Lord.

Hargrove, B. (1983). "Family in the White American Protestant Experience." In W. D. D'Antonio and J. Aldous eds., *Families and Religion: Conflict and Change in Modern Society* (pp. 113-140). Beverly Hills: SAGE.

Heggen, C. H. (1989). "Dominance/Submission Role Beliefs, Self-esteem and Self-acceptance in Christian Laywomen." Unpublished doctoral dissertation, University of New Mexico.

Heitritter, L., and J. Vought, (1989). *Helping Victims of Sexual Abuse: A Sensitive, Biblical Guide for Counselors, Victims and Families*. Minneapolis: Bethany House.

Hendrix, H. (1988). *Getting the Love You Want: A Guide for Couples*. New York: Harper and Row.

Herman, J., and L. Hirschman, (1981). "Families at Risk for Father-Daughter Incest." *American Journal of Psychiatry*, 138, 967-970.

Herman, J. L. (1981). *Father-Daughter Incest*. Cambridge, Mass.: Harvard University Press.

Howells, J. (1981). "Adult Sexual Interest in Children: Considerations Relevant to Theories of Etiology." In M. Cook and K. Howells (eds.), *Adult Sexual Interest in Children*. New York: Academic Press.

Hull, G. G. (1987). *Equal to Serve: Women and Men in the Church and the Home.* Old Tappan, N.J.: Fleming Revell.

Ingersoll, S. L., and S. O. Patton, (1990). *Treating Perpetrators of Sexual Abuse.* Lexington, Mass.: Lexington Books.

James, W. (1936). *The Varieties of Religious Experience.* New York: Modern Library.

LaHaye, B. (1980). *I Am a Woman by God's Design.* Old Tappan, N.J.: Fleming H. Revell.

LaHaye, T. (1990). *If Ministers Fall, Can They Be Restored?* Grand Rapids, Mich.: Zondervan.

Landis, J. (1956). "Experiences of 500 Children with Adult Sexual Deviants." *Psychiatric Quarterly Supplement, 30,* 91-109.

Laslett, P. (1972). *Household and Family in Past Time.* Cambridge, U.K.: Cambridge University Press.

Lebacqz, K., and R. G. Barton, (1991). *Sex in the Parish.* Louisville: Westminster/John Knox Press.

Lessin, R. (1979). *Spanking: Why, When, How?* Minneapolis: Bethany House Publishers.

Long, V. O., and C. H. Heggen, (1988). "Clergy Perceptions of Spiritual Health for Adults, Men, and Women." *Counseling and Values. 32* (3), 213-220.

Loss, P., and E. Glancy. Men Who Sexually Abuse Their Children. *Medical Aspects of Human Sexuality, 17,* 328-329.

Maltz, W., and B. Holman, (1987). *Incest and Sexuality: A Guide to Understanding and Healing.* Lexington, Mass.: Lexington Books.

McGuire, R. J., J. M. Carlisle, and B. G. Young (1965). "Sexual Deviations and Conditioned Behavior. A Hypothesis." *Behavior and Research Therapy, 2,* 185-190.

Miller, J. B. (1976). *Toward a New Psychology of Women.* Boston: Beacon Press.

Miller, P. (1976). "Blaming the Victim of Child Molestation: An Empirical Analysis." Unpublished doctoral dissertation, Northwestern University, Evanston, Ill.

Money, J. (1986). *Lovemaps: Clinical Concepts of Sexual/Erotic Health and Pathology, Paraphilia, and Gender Transposition in Childhood, Adolescence, and Maturity.* New York: Irvington.

Muck, T. C., ed. (1989). *Sins of the Body: Ministry in a Sexual Society.* Carol Stream, Ill.: Word.

Nelson, J. B. (1978). *Embodiment: An Approach to Sexuality and Christian Theology.* Minneapolis: Augsburg Publishing House.

Oswald, R., and O. Kroeger, (1988), *Personality Type and Religious Leadership.* Washington, D.C.: The Alban Institute.

Pancheri, P., and C. Benaissa, (1978). "Stress and Psychosomatic Illness." In C. Spielberger and I. Sarason (Eds.), *Stress and Anxiety,* Vol. 5. Washington, D.C.: Hemisphere.

Pelton, L. H., ed. (1981). *The Social Context of Child Abuse and Neglect.* New York: Human Sciences Press.

Peters, S. D. (1984). "The Relationship Between Childhood Sexual Victimization and Adult Depression Among Afro-American and White Women." Unpublished doctoral dissertation, University of California at Los Angeles.

Rohr, R., and A. Ebert, (1990). *Discovering the Enneagram*. New York: Crossroad.

Ruether, R., ed. (1974). *Religion and Sexism: Images of Woman in the Jewish and Christian Traditions*. New York: Simon and Schuster.

Rush, F. (1980). *The Best Kept Secret: Sexual Abuse of Children*. New York: McGraw-Hill.

Russell, D. E. H. (1982). *Rape in Marriage*. New York: Macmillan.

_____ (1983). "The Incidence and Prevalence of Intrafamilial and Extrafamilial Sexual Abuse of Female Children." *Child Abuse and Neglect, 7*, 133-146.

_____ (1984). "The Prevalence and Seriousness of Incestuous Abuse: Stepfathers vs. Biological Fathers." *Child Abuse and Neglect, 8*, 15-22.

_____ (1986). *The Secret Trauma: Incest in the Lives of Girls and Women*. New York: Basic Books.

Rutter, P. (1989). *Sex in the Forbidden Zone: When Men in Power—Therapists, Doctors, Clergy, Teachers, and Others—Betray Women's Trust*. Los Angeles: Jeremy P. Tarcher.

Salter, A. C. (1988). *Treating Child Sex Offenders and Victims: A Practical Guide*. Newbury Park, Calif.: SAGE.

Smedes, L. B. (1984). *Forgive and Forget: Healing the Hurts We Don't Deserve*. San Francisco: Harper and Row.

Smith, J. (1989). *Misogynies: Reflections of Myths and Malice*. New York: Fawcett Columbine.

Stoller, R. J. (1964). "A Contribution to the Study of Gender Identity." *International Journal of Psycho-Analysis, 45*, 220-226.

Swartley, W. M. (1983). *Slavery, Sabbath, War, and Women*. Scottdale, Pa.: Herald Press.

Trible, P. (1978). *God and the Rhetoric of Sexuality*. (Overtures to Biblical Theology Series). Philadelphia: Fortress.

_____ (1984). *Texts of Terror: Literary-Feminist Readings of Biblical Narratives*. Philadelphia, Pa.: Fortress Press.

Van Leeuwen, M. S. (1990). *Gender and Grace: Love, Work and Parenting in a Changing World*. Downers Grove, Ill.: InterVarsity Press.

Vine, W. E. (1985). *An Expository Dictionary of Biblical Words*. Nashville: Thomas Nelson.

Witmer, J., C. Rich, R. S. Barcikowski, and I. C. Mague, (1983). Psychosocial Characteristics Mediating the Stress Response: An Exploratory Study. *The Personnel and Guidance Journal, 62*. 73-77.

# The Author

Carolyn Holderread Heggen is a psychotherapist in Albuquerque and she specializes in treatment of adult survivors of sexual abuse. She is also on the graduate school faculty of Webster University, where she teaches in the counselor training program.

Heggen studied at Hesston (Kan.) College and received B.A. and M.A. degrees from Oregon State University. She received a Ph.D. in counseling from the University of New Mexico in 1989.

Heggen is a frequent lecturer and workshop leader. She speaks on issues related to human sexuality, the relationship between religious beliefs and mental health, and the prevention of domestic and pastoral abuse. She has extensive cross-cultural experience and has lived, worked, and done research in Latin America, India, and Pakistan.

Carolyn lives in New Mexico with her husband, Richard, a professor and string band musician, and their three children

—Melissa (1976), Amanda (1979), and Mark (1982). Playing French horn, cello, string bass, piano, and drum, they form an enthusiastic quintet (which has yet to cut an album). They are active members of Albuquerque Mennonite Church, where Carolyn serves as pastoral elder.